The Complete Cryptocurrency Investor's Book Bundle

2 Manuscripts

By Phillip J. Westbrook

The Complete Cryptocurrency Investor's Book Bundle

Book 1:

How to Make a Fortune in Cryptocurrencies By Investing in ICO's & Altcoins

By: Phillip J. Westbrook

The Complete Cryptocurrency Investor's Book Bundle

© Copyright 2018-2019 by Phillip J. Westbrook. All Rights Reserved

The following eBook is reproduced below with the goal of

providing information that is as accurate and reliable as possible. Regardless, purchasing this book can be seen as consent to the fact that both the publisher and the author of this book are in no way experts on the topics discussed within and that any recommendations or suggestions that are made herein are for entertainment purposes only. Professionals should be consulted as needed prior to undertaking any of the action endorsed herein.

This declaration is deemed fair and valid by both the American Bar Association and the Committee of Publishers Association and is legally binding throughout the United States.

Furthermore, the transmission, duplication or reproduction of any of the following work including specific information will be considered an illegal act irrespective of if it is done electronically or in print. This extends to creating a secondary or tertiary copy of the work or a recorded copy and is only allowed with express written consent from the Publisher. All additional right reserved.

The information in the following pages is broadly considered to be a truthful and accurate account of facts and as such any inattention, use or misuse of the information in question by the reader will render any resulting actions solely under their purview. There are no scenarios in which the publisher or the original author of this work can be in any fashion deemed liable for any hardship or damages that may befall them after undertaking information described herein.

Additionally, the information in the following pages is intended only for informational purposes and should thus be thought of as universal. As befitting its nature, it is presented without assurance regarding its prolonged validity or interim quality. Trademarks that are mentioned are done without written consent and can in no way be considered an endorsement from the trademark holder.

The Complete Cryptocurrency Investor's Book Bundle

Introduction

Congratulations on purchasing *How to Make a Fortune Investing in ICOs and Altcoins: A Guide to Making Money from Initial Coin Offerings, and other Cryptocurrencies such as Ethereum, Litecoin, Ripple and More* and thank you for doing so. After the insane jumps that Bitcoin experienced at the end of 2017, it is only natural that you are interested in taking the leap onto the cryptocurrency bandwagon yourself. As the price of bitcoin is currently drifting between $8,000 and $10,000 per unit, it is also perfectly natural that you would be interested in finding something a little friendlier on your wallet, but that is nevertheless full of all the same potential for future profits.

This is where altcoins and ICOs (initial coin offerings) come into play. There are more than 1,000 different cryptocurrencies on the market and more are coming online every day which means there are plenty of opportunities to make a quick buck or to lose your shirt if you choose poorly. While this can make it difficult to separate the wheat from the chaff, it also means that it can be very productive if you do so successfully. As such, the following chapters will teach you everything you need to know to help you choose your cryptocurrency investments wisely.

First, you will learn all about the basics surrounding initial coin offerings, alternatives to Bitcoin, known as altcoins, as well as some of what is currently taking place in the blockchain space. With your feet on the ground you will then learn about the risks and potential rewards that come from investing in ICOs. From there, you will learn about how investing in altcoins different from investing in ICOs and the ways in which this makes for a safer, if less flashy, investment. Finally, you will learn about many of the most popular altcoins on the market today including Ethereum, Ripple, Litecoin, Monero and more.

Without further ado, let's get started on your journey to making a fortune in cryptocurrency. This is so much bigger than bitcoin.

Chapter 1: The Bigger Picture

While Bitcoin was the major name in the cryptocurrency space for nearly a decade, 2018 looks poised to challenge that association more than ever before. There are more than 1,000 different cryptocurrencies on the market as of February 2018, with more being created practically every day. This means there are both alternatives to Bitcoin on the market already worth pursuing and that it may be worth keeping an eye on those that are still maturing as well.

Initial Coin Offerings (ICO's)

The idea for the initial coin offering comes from the initial public offering that more established companies go through when they are planning to issue stock for the first time. With the initial coin offering, a startup cryptocurrency is able to generate an, often significant, amount of capital by selling a new cryptocurrency at a very low price in hopes of attracting interest from speculative investors who are typically able to pay with cash as well as with other types of cryptocurrency. If the new cryptocurrency takes off in a big way, these early investors stand to make a significant amount of profit as a result.

While they share a naming convention, the fact of the matter is that the ICO is significantly different than the IPO which is an extremely measured process, with plenty of red tape at virtually every turn. When participating in an IPO, new investors receive equity for their cash, along with ownership shares and possibly voting rights as well, depending on the type of stock they are purchasing. This process is watched extremely closely, and, most importantly, overseen directly by the Securities and Exchange Commission.

There is none of this regulation when it comes to investing in ICOs, however, and the amount of information that is even available regarding the project that the cryptocurrency is funding will vary dramatically between projects. Regardless, investors should not expect to have any say over how the company develops, as all they are earning by investing early is access to units of the cryptocurrency at rates that are going to (hopefully) be lower than they ever will be again. Investors stand to have a giant potential payoff if the cryptocurrency does well after the ICO.

Those who have found success with ICOs in the past, or who are very positive on cryptocurrency in general, can argue that the process is like an accelerated version of venture capitalism and point to success in the market such as Ethereum to back them up. If you haven't heard of Ethereum, it is likely the second biggest name in the cryptocurrency space in 2018. While Bitcoin focuses almost exclusively on P2P payment transactions, Ethereum has instead focused on creating a platform for people to utilize smart contracts to the fullest. While Ethereum is discussed in detail in a later chapter, suffice it to say that it has done quite a bit for the cryptocurrency world since its inception in 2013.

You may be interested to know that Ethereum in fact was funded through what today would be called an ICO. The online crowd sale for its currency, ether, took place in the summer of 2014 and the cryptocurrency launched in 2015 with nearly 12 million coins presold. Today, that number accounts for slightly more than 10 percent of the total number of ether in circulation.

    A more recent example would be Wanchain, which was founded by one of the cofounders of Factom, which itself is currently worth an estimated $200 million. In addition to offering its own cryptocurrency, wancoin, Wanchain offers up the unique ability to easily connect to a wide variety of different blockchains, making true interoperability in the cryptocurrency space possible. Wanchain ran its ICO in October of 2017 and sold all 210,000,000 of its early access coins for a total of $36 million. Wanchain will also be discussed in detail in a later chapter.

The very first ICO was held in 2012 when the creator of Mastercoin released a whitepaper detailing the ways he felt that blockchain technology could be used for more than just cryptocurrencies. In his whitepaper he also asked that anyone who liked what he had to say send him one bitcoin ($100 USD at the time) in exchange he would provide them with 100 Mastercoins. As of February 2018, 1 Mastercoin is worth about $4.20. The plea worked and Mastercoin was funded via approximately 5,000 bitcoins, worth more than $50 million in 2018.

A typical ICO example: The average ICO is going to begin with a whitepaper that serves to outline the budget for the project, along with its goals, the technical specifics of what sets it apart from its competition and a project plan with a timeline for implementation and a discussion of how the coins will be released. The average new ICO is going to set a specific number of coins that will be released, prior to the start of the sale. While each investor might be only able to invest a specific amount of money, the price of the new coin will change as the ICO progresses so that those who get in during the opening minutes will end up with more coins than those who got in just before things shut down.

This is not guaranteed, however, as it is also possible for new coins to be generated throughout the ICO so that everyone who wants to buy in has the ability to do so on an even playing field. Likewise, some ICOs will take place through a third-party service while others will take place on a private website that is managed by the company issuing the cryptocurrency. While both options have produced numerous successful results over the years, these days the more credible offerings typically take place on a popular exchange or through an escrow service to ensure things are on the up and up as much as possible.

Altcoin basics

An altcoin is any cryptocurrency besides Bitcoin. You see, despite its flaws, Bitcoin still makes up more than 50 percent of the total cryptocurrency market cap which makes anything else, even major contenders like Ethereum and Litecoin, upstarts that are aiming at the king. To understand why you might be interested in investing in one or more of these altcoins, the first thing you need to understand is why they exist in the first place.

First and foremost, it is important to understand that while Bitcoin was the first cryptocurrency to market, it is far from perfect. New blocks in the Bitcoin blockchain can only be produced every 10 minutes, which means that even if no new bitcoin transactions were completed until it was caught up, the blockchain would need more than a week to catch up with all of the transactions that are currently waiting to be processed.

Additionally, the proof of work mining model uses an extreme amount of computing power, currently each transaction requires enough energy to run the average American home for several days. Finally, there will only ever be about 21 million bitcoins, with most of those having been mined during the early days of the cryptocurrency. These things were all conscious choices that the person who created Bitcoin, the alias Satoshi Nakamoto, made, based on usage case for their creation that was significantly less massive in scope than it has ultimately become.

While there is nothing to say that they can't make dramatic changes, those who have since become the curators of Bitcoin have proven extremely hesitant to make any changes to the source code of the blockchain. However, this is largely to protect the investments of those who own large amounts of the coin, frequently millions of dollars worth, this is understandable. Nevertheless, the core Bitcoin blockchain code is opensource which means other developers, with nothing on the line, have been able to adapt the original code in a variety of interesting ways. Popular Altcoins in 2018 include Ethereum, Litecoin,

Ripple, IOTA, Zcash, Neo and Steem.

Most altcoins improve on the core of the bitcoin blockchain technology by improving the speed at which new blocks are created and its overall stability and security as well. Many are trying alternatives to the standard proof-of-work mining process that Bitcoin pioneered, by either tweaking the difficultly of the mining process or trying an entirely different verification system instead.

As there are so many different altcoins on the market, the possibility of falling for a scamcoin is unfortunately high as well. Scamcoins, as the name implies, are a type of altcoin that is created purely for the profit of its creator. It will never amount to much of anything and will only ever decrease in value from wherever it started. As it can be difficult to tell the two apart when the coin is just finding its feet, it is very important to always do your homework before investing in anything and to never, ever, invest more than you can afford to lose.

Telling a good coin from a bad coin: In general, the best way to ensure the coin you are investing in isn't some developer's get rich quick scheme is to ensure that it has either significantly altered the original blockchain code, does something uniquely productive or has a specific application. Essentially, it is going to need a reason to exist outside of the fact that it is an alternate to fiat currency, before you should consider going anywhere near it.

Furthermore, you are going to want to stick to altcoins that have proven teams behind them. While the mainstream is just coming around on cryptocurrency, Bitcoin will celebrate its tenth birthday in 2019 which means there are plenty of names in the industry that have helped to build it, literally, from the ground up. While you may not be familiar with them, you can bet that those who are going to be investing will which means it will be extremely easy to attach names to previous success stories. On the other hand, you are also going to want to be on the lookout for altcoins whose team has no record whatsoever in the community as they likely don't have the experience to create something that is going to succeed in the long-term.

Unpredictable: Finally, when it comes to getting into the altcoin market for the first time, it is important to keep in mind that, oftentimes, the market is going to be downright unpredictable. Take Dogecoin, for example. The dogecoin features a likeness of the Siba Inu dog from the doge internet meme that was extremely popular in 2013. Due to a successful crowdfunding campaign, a solid gold dodgecoin is on track to be sent to the moon in 2019. While it was first introduced as somewhat of a joke, hence the meme logo, it rapidly developed an online following and reached a capitalization of greater than $60 million in less than a month. What sets it apart from other cryptocurrencies is its rapid coin production schedule and in its first year and a half 100 million coins were produced. It is most commonly uses as a means for social media users to tip one another when particularly noteworthy content is provided.

When it was first created, there was no doubt in anyone's mind that it was a joke that would burn out alongside the meme that inspired it. However, for a brief period of time, it was one of the most profitable cryptocurrencies to own and it is likely that more than one person was able to buy a house based on $100 they threw at the internet as a joke. This is not to demean altcoins in any way, and indeed, cryptocurrency is likely to go down as the most important technology created this decade. Instead, it is simply to point out that many parts of the cryptocurrency market may as well be the wild west which means that sometimes you will just have to expect the unexpected.

Blockchain Innovations

For those who are unaware, blockchain technology was created at the same time as Bitcoin and is at the heart of all cryptocurrency technology. It is essentially a decentralized ledger that allows for the simultaneous storage of data from users spread out all around the world. Each blockchain is made up of individual blocks that are filled with unique information as well as information related to where they exist on the chain, making it easy for data to stay in order regardless of when, or where, it is uploaded to the rest of the chain. All of this data is timestamped and also secured in such a way that it is virtually impenetrable using existing technology.

The benefits of blockchain technology extend far beyond financial transactions and virtually every industry in the world is currently looking for ways to make blockchain technology work for them in new and exciting ways. While blockchain technology is already synonymous with cryptocurrency payments, the fact of the matter is that more can be done in that space to facilitate the needs of businesses when it comes to utilizing blockchain to its fullest potential. The Ethereum Enterprise Alliance is a group of major corporations such as Microsoft, JP Morgan and Samsung that are working together to build a blockchain that is based on Ethereum technology but also contains the level of control that businesses would need in order to use the technology on a regular basis.

This type of service, while extremely common in some parts of the world, is extremely hard to come by in others. As such, more people in Kenya currently have a bitcoin wallet than have indoor plumbing. Connecting all these new individuals to the internet is going to have serious ramifications for retailers worldwide.

Another important, yet often overlooked cost to businesses is fraud which cost business owners an estimated $20 billion in 2017. Broken down, this means that nearly 30 % of all profits are going to end up dealing with some type of fraudulent activity. Blockchain technology has the potential to decrease this amount substantially as it can make tracking digital identities far easier than was previously the case as its results are always going to be properly authenticated, irrefutable and immutable. If this type of system were to become widespread then it would make it much easier for everyone to remain safe and accounted for.

Finally, one of the industries likely to see the most benefit from blockchain technology, outside of the financial industry, is likely going to be supply chain logistics. If there is one thing that companies have long proven they are unable to do reliably, it's conveying communication across multiple different systems. Blockchain technology, on the other hand, makes this type of tracking practically child's play and eventually even customers will be able to track all of their purchases from the manufacturing all the way to their doorstep.

Chapter 2: Investing in ICOs

While a majority of the funding for existing ICOs has come from Asia thus far, there are investors worldwide who have jumped on board the ICO train. It should be noted, however, that if investing in traditional cryptocurrency is a risky proposition, then investing in ICOs is even more so. There are several different reasons that this is the case. One of the biggest potential issues is that the companies that frequently offer this type of incentive are barely up and running which means they aren't going to have much to show in terms of prototypes. Some of them may not even offer a business plan.

When doing your research first you will want to find their website, whitepaper, and business plan to pull information from. Obviously not all ICO's are created equally. Some of them will feel like successful startups poised for their IPO where you can readily find all the information you need to make an informed investment. Others may not even have a website or business plan to offer. This doesn't mean they aren't investible per se, but you should be very wary ICO's that have little to no available information. Furthermore, you are going to want to keep in mind that just because a company is seeing a strong response to their plan, doesn't necessarily mean this hype will directly translate to sales. Even worse, many analysts are of the opinion that giving a new company too much money too soon will only cause them to feel the need to spend it all while also minimizing the importance of actually producing a quality product because they are already seeing the fruits of their labor.

The informed investor will be aware of these risks and enter into a transaction with eyes wide open. While getting in on the ground floor of a new cryptocurrency is undeniably the best way to get the best possible deal on a potentially viable investment, there is a risk that the cryptocurrency won't amount to anything in either the short or the long-term as well. Don't forget, ICOs aren't regulated in the same way as IPOs which means that you are going to need to work harder to ensure that everything is on the level.

Evaluate an ICO

While there are many ICOs out there that never amounted to anything more than another useless token a good amount of tokens have achieved amazing success for investors. The Ethereum Token which raised a staggering $18.4 million during its own ICO is just one of the many examples. There are plenty, like Ethereum, that have gone on to shake the foundation of the cryptocurrency world. The key then lies, of course, in being able to tell the difference between the coins that will skyrocket and those that will crash and burn.

Here are some useful steps to get started in evaluating a coin:

Look at the development team: Regardless of whether the ICO you are interested in has a charismatic figurehead, you are going to want to dig deeper into their team composition before putting your money on the line. This means you are going to want to look up the resume of each and every person on the team and see what they have done before and do the same for the advisory board as well. While you don't need to already be familiar with their names, you need to be on the lookout for project names that you recognize (the more the merrier). The greater the number of successful projects the team has under its belt, the greater the odds of it actually seeing the light of day in a usable form.

Look for buzz in the community: Depending on where you hear about the ICO in question, you are going to want to determine if there is buzz surrounding it in the community at the moment. While early buzz isn't necessarily indicative of eventual sale when the project is up and running, it is at least a good sign that someone besides you is interested in the upcoming ICO. Afterall, the coin is relying on potential investors like you to fund their ICO so if there's a lot of hype in the community about the coin, that's a good indicator that this is a coin you should pay attention to. Even if there's nothing revolutionary about the coin, the mere fact that people are excited about it means they may be willing to invest in it which means the value of that coin will rise with its popularity.

One of the best places to go for this type of information is BitcoinTalk.org. It is the biggest cryptocurrency forum online as of 2018, and any ICO of note is almost certainly going to have their own announcement thread there. When looking through these sorts of threads, you are going to want to read all of the comments, no matter how inane many of them might ultimately be.

These message boards will provide you with plenty of details regarding the ICO that you will be unlikely to find anywhere else. It will also provide you with one of the earliest opportunities to talk to the people directly behind the cryptocurrency in question. Getting a feel for the coin from its creator will give you a better idea of how it will expand if it catches on in the mainstream.

Most importantly, however, this message board will serve as a microcosm of what people seem to think about the ICO in general. As such, it is important to not disregard every negative comment out of hand, and instead read them thoroughly on the off chance that they present a valid argument that could ultimately save you money. Furthermore, while a few negative comments are nothing to worry about, if you find that the announcement thread is full of more negative comments than positive ones it is a pretty clear sign that the ICO doesn't have very much public support. If the buzz around the cryptocurrency isn't positive at this early stage in the game, then it is unlikely it will ever be unless something significant changes in the coin itself or in the market.

It is important to ensure that this buzz isn't artificially generated. ICOs have been known to offer coins to community members who make it seem as though there is extra buzz surrounding the ICO in question. The easiest way to see if this type of buzz is building is to search for the ICO in question with the word bounty after it. If there is a Twitter, Facebook or Reddit bounty on the ICO then this should be enough to find it. You should also be on the lookout for multiple people posting almost the same type of post as this can be a sign that all those accounts are working from the same script.

Consider the state of the project: Before you put your money into any new ICO it is important to take a good look at how close the project it is funding is to fruition. A version of the software running in a limited beta is best, though a prototype can still be acceptable in some cases. A vast majority of ICOs are only going to have a whitepaper, a song and a prayer, though a considerable number of these have achieved wild success as well, so there are more important things than having something tangible to show for the money you are putting in.

This is what makes investing in an ICO somewhat similar to investing in a venture capital opportunity. However, in the case of venture capitalism, or investing in a business, shares of ownership are typically exchanged. It's all about finding the right level of risk for you and then having the ability to know when you have found a project that is worth pulling the trigger over. In fact, there are several cryptocurrency venture capital firms currently in operation, including Fenbushi which is owned by Ethereum founder Vitalik Buterin. Seeing one of these names attached to an ICO should make you feel much more confident when it comes to pulling the trigger.

Consider their community presence: While this might not always exist at the time you are getting involved with a specific cryptocurrency, it is important to keep an eye on how the community around the

ICO grows over time. A supportive, committed community is crucial to ensuring the success in the long-term. Likewise, it is important to ensure that the developers maintain strong communication with early investors to ensure that everyone always remains on the same page at all time. It is important to keep the overall atmosphere of this community in mind and also to ensure that its numbers continuously trend in a positive direction.

Consider the demand for the service in question: Ideally, you won't touch any ICO that doesn't have a valid reason, in theory at least, to exist. If the whitepaper doesn't go into significant detail about some problem that only this new type of blockchain technology or cryptocurrency can fix, then you have to wonder why it is being created in the first place. Assuming the ICO gets this far at least, then the next thing that you are going to want to do is to do your homework and see what the demand is actually like out in the real world.

To do so you are going to turn to the internet and run searches related to solving the problem discussed in the whitepaper in question. If the goal of the project is to create a cryptocurrency that can be used by dentists and their patients in lieu of traditional insurance, for example, then you would want to look into how dentistry options are handle in different countries and how common international options are considered.

In addition to ensuring that the goal of the cryptocurrency or blockchain project that you are funding is going to fill a real need, that real people are going to be interested in dealing with in a new way, it is important to ensure that the cryptocurrency itself is going to legitimately be a part of the process. Unless you can come up with a decent reason for the project in question to not just use an existing coin, besides the promised payout of an ICO, then you should likely stay as far away from it as possible. Remember, a cryptocurrency is only worth what other people are willing to pay for it and if no one is interested in using it, besides those who bought in early, then the price is never going to go anywhere but down.

Consider the cap on the cryptocurrency: In the early days of ICOs the amount of coins that were ultimately going to be generated when the cryptocurrency was up and running wasn't all that important. Many ICOs get bought out in seconds these days, however, so knowing what you are competing for is an important part of the process. An open cap, meaning that an unlimited number of people can put in an unlimited amount of money up front, is useful in that it makes it easier for everyone who is interested in getting the cryptocurrency to pick it up for the cheapest price possible.

It also makes the cryptocurrency fair less unique overall which means that it is going to start at a lower price overall than might otherwise be the case. This is especially important to keep in mind as it means it is going to be more difficult to make money early on, which may very well be the only time the cryptocurrency in question is profitable. For example, the blockchain company Bancor ran an ICO in the summer of 2017 that raised $150 million in under three hours. Despite this impressive number, the investors at the time saw zero gain as the amount of cryptocurrency for sale was unlimited.

On the other hand, if the cryptocurrency in question is going to have a hard cap then there is only so many coins available during the ICO and each person is only allowed a specific amount. While you have to be much more on the ball with this type of scenario, the end result is that you have a cryptocurrency that is worth far more than it would otherwise be during the early days of trading.

Consider how the tokens are going to be distributed: When it comes to determining how any cryptocurrency tokens you buy are going to be distributed, it is important that you understand not just how you will receive your tokens, but when as well. Some project release their tokens as soon as the ICO ends while some projects won't even have the capability of sending out tokens until they have spent most of the money that was earned from selling them in the first place. While sometimes this can create additional hype around the project, which is what happened with Ethereum, this delay in momentum is just as likely to hurt the new project as it is to help it.

It is also important to pay close attention to the percentage of the coins that are going to be created during the ICO are going to go to those who are buying in as opposed to those that are going to the development team. If the team is getting 50 percent or more of all the coins at launch then this is a likely sign that they may be doing so just to make a quick buck as opposed to actually creating anything that has a lasting value, much less something that will reward its early investors with additional profits. As such, this is a great way to get a look at the true motivations of the team behind the ICO, regardless of how chivalrous their whitepaper might seem.

Consider the whitepaper: While this shouldn't need to be said, studies show that less than 40 percent of all investors read the whitepapers of their investments completely, so it is worth repeating. Remember, this can be considered a roadmap of where your entire investment is going both in the short-term and the long-term which means that not reading through it thoroughly is akin to gambling with your investment capital and if you plan on gambling there are far more lucrative ways of doing so than investing in cryptocurrency.

As the whitepaper is naturally going to be the best-case scenario for the project in question, it is important to read it with a grain of salt. Nevertheless, you should still be able to pick out the most important facts about the project and understand how the goals discussed within can be brought to fruition in a way that makes other people legitimately interested in using the cryptocurrency that you will be buying into. After reading the whitepaper you should be able to determine not only what type of value the project adds to the world but how the development team will go about making it a reality and why it is likely to succeed despite the competition in the market.

Consider the quality of the code: While you don't need to be able to program yourself, you are still going to want to take a long hard look at what other programmers think of the source code for the project before you go anywhere near it. Luckily, all blockchain code thus far has been released in an opensource fashion, dating all the way back to the original blockchain code. It is still sitting on GitHub.com, waiting for anyone who is interested to use it in any way they see fit. While you are there, you are going to want to look up the ICO in question because you should be able to easily find it on the site as well.

While there, you are going to want to read the comments of those who do understand the code, to ensure that people who know what they are talking about believe that it is solid. Again, you don't need to be worried about every single negative comment, just the trends that they appear to be creating as if 20 people comment on the same issue then maybe it is worth looking into. The people on GitHub likely have nothing to lose, they are simply commenting on the code as they see it which means they can be an extremely effective judge of the overall quality of a potential project.

Chapter 3: Investing in Altcoins

While the actual process of investing in altcoins isn't much different than investing in stocks, the differences between the two are still significant enough that the process can be confusing if you don't know what you are in for. When you buy into a cryptocurrency, you aren't purchasing anything physical, such as share of a company, instead you are buying digital tokens from a third party that everyone agrees has some value compared to more traditional fiat currencies. To complicate things further, cryptocurrencies typically have both a transactional purpose, what the coin was originally created to do, along with a speculative purpose which is strengthened if it catches on for investment purposes. Understanding both values is crucial to your long-term cryptocurrency investment success.

Another thing that is important to keep in mind is that while the conversation around cryptocurrency makes it seem as though everyone who is anyone is buying in at a fantastic rate, the reality is that only an extremely small portion of the population owns any cryptocurrency, much less interacts with it on a regular basis. What this means for you, the person who is considering purchasing cryptocurrency in the spring of 2018, is that there is very much still plenty of opportunity to get in on the ground floor of the cryptocurrencies that will be hitting $100 or more in 2019 and beyond.

As such, when the true usage rate is compared to the current $650 billion market cap, and the amount of buzz surrounding them, the altcoin future, as a whole, seems exceedingly bright. This means that while there is no arguing that the overall volatility rate of a specific altcoin, sometimes as high as 15 times the volatility of investing in the S&P 500, is quite high, its long-term prospects are largely positive, assuming of course that it can make it past the mass saturation point.

Mass saturation point: When investing in altcoins, one of the first things you are always going to want to keep in mind is the coming promise of the mass saturation point. The mass saturation point is the point where a majority of the population is using cryptocurrency of some type for the first time. While notable for what it means for the future of fiat currency, it is also likely to signal the beginning of the end for the pricing bubble that has surrounded cryptocurrency since its inception.

Right from the start, Bitcoin had issues with pricing bubbles, simply because there were always more people interested in buying the cryptocurrency and holding onto it for speculative purposes rather than trading it back and forth for normal transactions. As such, the value was driven above what pure market value would dictate and a bubble formed. Every form of cryptocurrency is subject to this aspect of the market to one degree or another, and it is important to know how much your cryptocurrency of choice is being affected by such things when you buy in for the first time.

However, this will cease to be the case when the mass saturation point hits as, for the first time, the market will likely be full of as many people actually using their cryptocurrency as hording it. While this will be great for those who go in early and didn't lose more than what they bought in at, this will certainly not be the case for those who buy in late. The results will likely mimic the dotcom crash of the late 1990s with the strongest companies surviving and the hundreds of weaker alternatives disappearing to never be heard from again. This is why it is important to invest in cryptocurrencies with a high degree of demonstrable value as they are far more likely to make it through the crash than those that are simply a boring clone of Bitcoin.

Choose the right investment for you: Before doing anything else, the first thing you are going to want to do is consider which cryptocurrency is right for you, which means thinking about what each altcoin brings to the table. For starters, this means choosing something that is in your price range, while at the same time giving you a higher than average number of shares per dollar. For example, if you have $2,000 to invest, buying a fifth of a bitcoin isn't going to do you nearly as much good as buying 2,000 units of Ripple of 4,000 units of lumens. If you plan for volatility, then you can make it your friend; for example, if Ripple was priced at $1, then a $1 increase is perfectly reasonable to expect from a cryptocurrency which means that you just made $2,000 on a $2,000 investment, in a single day. Stick with cheaper shares of smaller cryptocurrencies and you will see the most bang for your buck overall.

In this example, it is important to note the cryptocurrencies that were mentioned both have clear and compelling reasons as to why they make investment sense in both the short and the long-term. Ripple is used to facilitate a variety of transactions between businesses and lumens were designed to give those in third world countries greater access to banking services. Both of these services have clear demands from the market and serve to solve an existing problem in the process. As such, you could invest in either of the examples and be relatively confident that they will survive the inevitable mass saturation point. Choosing a cryptocurrency that has a well-defined reason for being is crucial to your long-term investing success. Remember, the more useful the better.

Choose an exchange that matches your plan: When it comes to trading in altcoins, it is important to determine right away if you plan on investing large sums all at once, or if you are going to be making smaller, steadier investments over time. This is especially important as you are going to want to ensure that the exchange you ultimately choose is going to offer rates that are in line with your how you plan on moving forward. If you plan on making numerous, smaller transactions then you are going to want to find an exchange that offers transactions rates based on a percentage of what the total of the transaction is. If you are going to be making fewer, larger transactions, then you will want to find an exchange that offers flat rates. Don't forget, you will likely have to verify your account after you join a new exchange, which can take several days. This is not the case if you start with some type of cryptocurrency in your possession as then there is rarely any type of verification process required.

Spread the love: After you have found one type of cryptocurrency that works for you and you get a general feel for the marketplace overall, the next thing you are going to want to do is to diversify your investment. Don't forget, regardless of how your chosen cryptocurrency investment does in the short-term, it is still an extremely volatile investment which means that you are going to want to do everything in your power to limit the risk you are exposing yourself too as much as possible. As such, rather than reinvesting any early earnings you might have had back into your primary cryptocurrency, it makes far more sense to instead spread your investment to a second altcoin instead.

This is where creating a portfolio comes into play and it should be considered a crucial part of any long-term investment strategy. Diversifying is also useful in that it makes it far easier to protect your profits than it would be if your holdings were all tied up in a single type of cryptocurrency. This is due to the fact that it is unlikely that all of your investments are going to see a loss at the same time, saving you from going from all to nothing, all at once. When it comes to determining how you are going to distribute your money, you are going to want to keep in mind your current tolerance for risk, your level of familiarity when it comes to investing and how much time you are willing to spend micromanaging the investments that you do make.

When choosing a type of cryptocurrency to invest in as a secondary investment, it is important that you take a close look at its historical pricing data to ensure that you have a firm grasp on the types of patterns it is likely to run through on a regular, if not necessarily predictable, basis. Every cryptocurrency is going to move to its own rhythms and understanding the ins and out of each cryptocurrency you choose is going to be key when it comes to making the right decisions about the future when everything suddenly changes. If you plan on investing in the long-term then you can expect these types of dips from time to time, and they will be nothing to worry about. However, occasionally they will represent a more clear and present danger and you will want to do everything you can to learn the relevant patterns, so you can easily tell the difference.

Invest in the right way: When investing in altcoins, it can be easy to jump after short-term profits as it can be difficult to predict, if, or when, the current price is going to come around again. As such, it is often better to take advantage of long-term strategies as doing so will make it far more likely that you will see success from your time spent with cryptocurrency when everything is said and done. The basic idea at play here has to do with compounding, coupled with the significant amount of movement most altcoins can see in an extremely short period of time.

The basic idea behind compounding is that reinvesting your early returns is the best, and most effective, means of maximizing your profits in the long run. Selling when the price is high and then buying in again when it has dropped allows you to do just that.

The idea behind compounding states that reinvesting your early returns is the best way to maximize your profits in the long run. To understand just how powerful compounding can be, consider a person in their mid-twenties who wanted to be a millionaire by the time they were 65. In order to make this dream a reality they would need to save an average of $900 per month, every month, between now and the day they retired, assuming they were earning a paltry (for bitcoin) five percent return on their investment per year. However, if this same person waited until they were in their mid-30s to start saving they would need to save about $2,200 each month, and if they waited 20 years to start saving regularly then they would need to save $4,500 each month to see the same result.

While many long-term investing plans make do with low, but reliable, yearly returns, to build their compounding capital over time, the volatility inherent with altcoins means that you can see the same results as several years of compounding via traditional investments in a far shorter period of time. This, in turn, significantly reduces the effectiveness of short-term trading with altcoins as the amount of movement you see in the short-term is rarely going to be large enough to justify the additional fees that will be paid with the additional trades that will be made pursuing this course of action.

Aside from getting started as soon as you possible can, you are also going to want to ensure that you are properly aware of your personal investment habits to make sure that you are helping, rather than hindering your investments. This means that you are going to want to keep in mind the fact that just because an investment strategy has proven effective for someone, doesn't mean that person is you. In general, you are going to want to keep in mind the level of risk that you are comfortable with as this is going to play a big part in whether you are successful in the long-term.

As you are planning to invest in cryptocurrency then you are clearly not completely averse to risk, however, there are still shades of gray that you will need to consider. Specifically, you will want to consider if you are more interested in keeping your investment capital in tact or risking it all in exchange for the biggest possible reward. The specifics of the plan you choose don't matter, what matters is that you are able to stick with the plan when the time comes. You are going to need to be able to rely on your plan in the heat of the moment, when every fiber of your being is telling you to go against it for one reason or another which means knowing yourself enough to know what you can do to ensure that you make the right decision when it matters most.

Additionally, when it comes to making your plan it is important to keep in mind that nothing that you are going to do will take place in a vacuum. This means you are going to want to keep in mind all the external factors that you will have to deal with that may be standing between you and your ideal altcoin trading scenario.

Finally, when it comes to deciding on how much you are going to spend on your new cryptocurrency investment adventure, it is important to keep in mind that you should never invest more than you can afford to lose. If you decide to invest money that you need for more pressing matters in a volatile cryptocurrency market, then you will never be able to look at your investment rationally and will always be concerned about protecting those funds. It is also important to factor in how long you anticipate holding the investment for as the more time you have, the more you will be able to let loose and take risks as you will have plenty of time to correct them if things don't work out.

This is especially true for those who have at least 20 years between now and the time they plan to retire. If you fall into this category then there is no reason you shouldn't go as hard on cryptocurrency investments of one type or another as possible as this amount of time means you will have plenty of chances to recoup early loss and make substantial profits as a result.

Chapter 4: Altcoins to Watch

Ripple: While the news at the end of 2017 focused almost exclusively on Bitcoin's extreme gains, at the same time Ripple was having quite a time of it as well. At the start of December 2017, it was worth about $0.25 and by the end of the month it was as high as $2.65. This extreme price increase led to it briefly having the greatest market cap of all non-Bitcoin cryptocurrencies. While most cryptocurrencies were up during this time, Ripple wasn't just coasting on the waves of good cheer surrounding cryptocurrency at the end of 2018, it was solidifying its place among the cryptocurrencies most likely to survive past the mass saturation point.

First, the beginning of the month marked the completion of a cryptographic lockup of all its tokens, making it as secure as it could possibly be given its underlying technology. Within a week of this milestone, it saw a dramatic increase from cryptocurrency exchanges across Asia, which kept its price moving in the right direction. This was in response to a then-vindicated rumor that saw a Tokyo-based firm announce that it was creating a Ripple consortium which would explore the many ways in which Ripple technology could be used as the basis for a cryptocurrency debit card.

Unlike most other cryptocurrency platforms, Ripple isn't used for standard transactions, rather it operates as a payment network for financial institutions and banks that makes it possible for them to complete transactions between themselves much more quickly than would otherwise be the case. Additionally, Ripple as a company is made up of three parts. Ripple Labs is the parent company, while RippleNet is the payment network that is being used to make payments and XRP (also called Ripple) is the cryptocurrency token that banks will be exchanging between themselves.

Like other blockchains, Ripple operates on a decentralized network of nodes with each node being attached to a bank or other financial organization. As the transactions that are being made aren't for standard transactional purposes, XRP can be thought of as something more akin to a settlement token than a representation of its own cryptocurrency. As money is not changing hands in a traditional way, Ripple transactions are also verified differently, which means that additional units are not created through the mining process either.

Instead, transactions are verified by multiple interested parties to ensure that a consensus is reached for every transaction. One hundred billion XRP were created at the launch of Ripple which represents the total amount of available Ripple. However, 60 billion of those are owned by Ripple Labs and are not included in the day-to-day Ripple valuation.

Another way that Ripple differs from other types of cryptocurrency is the fact that its speculative market does not directly affect the success of Ripple as a company. Instead, it can be thought of as speculative trading more in line with forex trading than anything else. What makes Ripple appealing to banks is that it gives them the ability to move a large amount of currency quickly, as Ripple transactions clear in seconds. Ripple was trading at about $0.80 per unit as of February 2018.

Litecoin: Litecoin is a P2P cryptocurrency that makes possible nearly instantaneous, low cost payments between individuals anywhere in the world. If you have ever heard the pitch for Bitcoin, then this all likely sounds the same and that's because it is. This is because Litecoin is built on the Bitcoin blockchain and, in fact, was originally designed so that it would function as the silver to Bitcoin's gold standard though the relationship between the two has cooled somewhat since as Litecoin began to eclipse Bitcoin in terms of functionality.

Litecoin is, in many respects, very similar to bitcoin, though it features some technical improvements as well. It allows for a much greater number of transactions to be processed over a shorter period of time which prevents the bottlenecks that are seen with bitcoin today. Its blocks are processed in approximately two and a half minutes as compared to bitcoin's ten-minute limit. This can lead to a higher number of orphaned blocks, however, though it also leads to a decreased chance of a double spending attack occurring. Overall, it requires approximately ten times less work from a computational standpoint to mine a litecoin block than a bitcoin block. It also offers very low payments costs and completes payments approximately four times faster than bitcoin does.

The most interesting aspect of Litecoin is the fact that it is the first of the five biggest cryptocurrencies by market cap to implement what is known as the Segregated Witness (Segwit) technology which was created as a way of increasing the overall size of the individual blocks that are stored in the blockchain, thus helping more blocks to be verified in an overall shorter period of time. This is done through a process of splitting transactions into two separate segments, removing the portion of the transaction that verifies the sender and moving it to the end of the transaction before counting it as a separate structure.

This allows the primary section of the transaction to retain the data consisting of sender and receiver data, while leaving the new witness structure to take care of any scripts and signatures that the block might contain. The primary section then retains its normal size, minus the missing bits, while the witness section is then compacted down to about 25 percent of its original size.

The biggest issue that bitcoin has to deal with is the fact that the original blockchain code it is running on has a hard limit when it comes to the amount of transactions that can be forced into a single block and also how fast each block can be added to the blockchain which is only once every 10 minutes. This, in turn, severely hampers the speed of the blockchain as a whole while also effectively adding a hard cap to the number of users who can use the service concurrently. This problem is then multiplied in areas with fewer nodes where users can easily wait an hour or more to have a single transaction verify successfully.

Litecoin runs on the scrypt proof of work model works which works similarly to the hashcash proof of work model, though with a different hash function at its source. It is a more memory intensive hash function which means that it functions more easily with a CPU mining machine than other types of cryptocurrencies that are GPU mining machine dominant. While GPU mining machines have since increased in power to the point that they are the best choice, regardless of the cryptocurrency in question, the sheer fact that the algorithm is used less frequently than hashcash automatically means that it is far less likely to be target by hackers.

The scrypt proof of work model does have a few extra issues of its own, however, starting with the fact that it requires fewer specialized systems in order to pull off a hack of the system, though this won't be done through a traditional 51 percent attack as the scrypt proof is immune to these types of attacks. Current estimates state that it would cost about $400 per megahash per second over a reliable network and would require a hashrate of 30 gigahashes per second. As such, the total estimated equipment to takeover and match the network would be roughly 12 million dollars. As of February 2018, 1 Litecoin is worth about $145.

Zcash: Zcash is a type of cryptocurrency that is primarily concerned with user privacy above all else. As with all cryptocurrency transactions, Zcash transactions are published on the Zcash blockchain. However, unlike most other cryptocurrencies, Zcash users are allowed to conceal details from their transactions including the receiver, sender and the amount of the transaction in question. Zcash has a fixed supply of 21 million units. First released in 2016, Zcash offers those who got in during the ICO a share of 20 percent of all the Zcash coins that are created until October 2020.

Unlike most cryptocurrencies which use a variation on the proof-of-work protocol, Zcash uses a unique protocol known as Zerocash which offers up two different types of cryptocurrency. Zerocash are completely anonymous, while basecoins are capable of being tracked as normal. Zerocash transactions are even verified without any details about the transaction coming to light. This is completed via a zero-knowledge proof called zk-SNARK which allows the parties in the transaction to verify it while at the same time not revealing any information about themselves.

By allowing users to retain their confidentiality in this way, the developers hope to have solved for what is known as fungibility, or the ability for all of their coins to be indistinguishable for one another. While fungibility isn't that important to the market as a whole yet, there are already products on the market that allow users to determine the previous uses, and therefore users, of a given cryptocurrency, laying bare years of supposedly private transactions. This is already being used by cryptocurrency exchanges to prevent the use of stolen coins and it can be used for far less benign uses as well, unless something like the zero-knowledge proof takes off in a big way.

Transactions that are made using increased security are known as shielded transactions, but it is important to understand that currently only about four percent of all Zcash transactions take advantage of this added security. This is due to the fact that many traditional cryptocurrency wallets don't support the underlying technology required to shield transactions in this way.

On the other end of the spectrum, Zcash also provides users with the ability to officially disclose that they are either the sender or receiver of a specific transaction, allowing them to prove their connection to a specific Zcash account for auditing purposes. Thus, Zcash is a useful alternative to many cryptocurrencies when it comes to governments looking for ways to prevent money laundering while also making it possible to make purely untraceable transactions as long as you have the correct technology.

Zcash made an especially large splash when it was released in 2016 as it was the first cryptocurrency to offer this level of extreme privacy. In fact, prices once reached as high as $1,000 per unit. Since its inception, however, its technology has not gained as widespread of acceptance as proponents may have hoped and the price has dropped since that time. One Zcash is worth about $340 as of February 2018.

Dash: Unlike many other altcoins, Dash doesn't want to do anything other than act as an alternative to fiat currency. Built on the bitcoin blockchain, with improvements to privacy and transaction speed thrown in, it was worth about $500 per unit as of February 2018 with a total of 18 million coins. Dash has a variable block reward which decreases at a 7.1 percent rate each year. The average block mining time is 2.5 minutes on the Dash blockchain, which makes it four times faster than Bitcoin. What sets it apart from other types of cryptocurrency, however, is that its transaction fee is negotiable.

Additional features of Dash include the ability to send a transaction as private (worth up to 1000 dash) by mixing your transaction in with numerous others being transacted at the same time. More interesting, however, is its instant send feature which sends transactions instantly, though high transactions fees apply. This is done by sending prioritized transactions to a set of masternodes that sit outside of the traditional blockchain and stand ready to complete transactions virtually as fast as they are started. In order to be listed as a masternode, users need to own a minimum of 1,000 dash coins, when new coins are created 45 percent go to masternodes and 45 percent go to miners with the rest going to fund development.

Additionally, 10 percent of all of the mining rewards from the dash mining process are set aside to be returned to the creators for the purpose of improving the cryptocurrency even more. Currently, much of this fund is being used to develop a use of a new point of sale software that is being targeted at emergent industries in the US that are looking for alternatives to traditional financial structures. Dash also allows its users to vote in order to determine what projects are going to be focused on next.

Monero: Monero is a cryptocurrency that was created in 2014 in an effort to fix certain flaws that the creator saw in the Bitcoin blockchain. Specifically, Monero obscures the details regarding each and every transaction that is made on its blockchain, including the details regarding the sender, the receiver and the amount of the transaction in question. This focus on privacy has somewhat hurt its reputation over the years as it has publicly attracted the attention of those who were interested in evading law enforcement.

Monero is based on the CryptoNote protocol and uses its proof-of-work hash to verify transactions. There are many differences between the Cryptonote Protocol and the Bitcoin blockchain protocol, primarily having to do with the way that transactions are obfuscated. Much like Zcash, Monero is fungible so that any unit is truly equal to all other units.

In addition to the standard level of obfuscation, Monero transactions also utilize what are know as ring signatures with every transaction. A ring signature mixes the true sender of each transaction in with a variety of other signatures, making it extremely difficult to establish a link between any specific user and any specific transaction. Finally, multiple stealth address are generated with each transaction, blocking out where the transaction is likely going as well as where its coming from.

As a consequence of this, Moreno features an opaque blockchain which is a dramatic change from nearly every other blockchain on the market today. As such, Monero is classified as a private blockchain that is optionally transparent. As a result of this, Monero wallets have a pair of keys, one called a view key and the other a spend key. View keys are used to provide transparency while spend keys are used for actually completing transactions. Monero was worth approximately $212 as of Feb. 2018.

IOTA: IOTA is a different take on distributed ledger technology that is looking to function as a core part of an expanded internet of things. Its coin is worth about $1.90 in February 2018. IOTA is similar to Ripple in that it doesn't involve mining, although it differs as it doesn't contain blocks in a traditional sense as well. Instead, users on the network are required to validate a pair of transactions in order to be able to conduct one of their own for free. While no one is paying any transaction fees, no one is receiving rewards for mining either. Additionally, it offers secure data transmission through the network. If a user establishes a communication channel between two devices, then data sent via this channel is both tamper proof and fully authenticated.

IOTA is mainly being targeted at the growth of the internet of things. Specifically, it serves as a settlement layer that increases the ease with which various systems can interact with one another. IOTA isn't built on a traditional blockchain, instead it operates within what is known as the tangle. The tangle is a new type of distributed ledger that works in place of a more traditional blockchain. Instead of being built from blocks, transactions that are stored within the Tangle are done so using what are known as edges. Each transaction is connected by edges to the two transactions that were verified in order to allow it to be processed.

As IOTA transactions are completed, the relevant proof-of-work models are generated at the same time, without the person who is trying to verify a transaction having to do anything to start the process. The Tangle uses the same hashcash proof at its root, the same that is used in most traditional blockchains, just with the difficulty of the required proof decreased dramatically. This factor is what allows it to be tuned towards the internet of things as it can be used by machines to automatically verify a wide variety of different types of information without any human input whatsoever.

Furthermore, because of its design, the Tangle protocol can scale to virtually any requirement. In fact, unlike a traditional blockchain, the more users who are taking advantage of the Tangle at the same time, the faster their transactions will all be processed. As each of these transactions includes a one-time signature, the Tangle protocol is also future proof as it is not vulnerable to the types of 51 percent attacks that more traditional blockchains need to be wary of. There are a total of nearly 2.8 million units of IOTA, all of which were created during the ICO for the cryptocurrency in 2015. Currently almost the entire amount are active in the market with less than two percent not being claimed by early investors.

Currently the city of Taipei Taiwan is partnering with IOTA in order to become one of the world's first smart cities. This promises to bring a wide variety of new features to residents, including the TangleID which will serve as a means of minimizing identity theft, while also being used for everything from storing commonly used government information to voting. The card is also going to be designed with sensors that provide the user with relevant local details including things like current pollution and humidity levels as well as light levels and temperature.

Ethereum: Ethereum is currently one of the most popular cryptocurrency platforms on the market today. Its cryptocurrency is known as ether and it is mainly used for payment of services on the Ethereum platform which includes extensive use of what are known as smart contracts as well as the Ethereum Virtual Machine which allows users to generate decentralized apps that other users can then take advantage of in exchange for ether. Ether also see a fair amount of speculative investment, though it has not yet reached the heights of its main competitor bitcoin.

Ethereum was conceived of by a programmer associated with bitcoin by the name of Vitalik Buterin and written about in a whitepaper discussing decentralized applications in fall of 2013. His original pitch was to add a scripting language to bitcoin but his thoughts fell on deaf ears so he set out on his own to do just that. By the start of 2014, Buterin had his team together and by July 2015, Ethereum as we know it today was ready to launch.

A big part of what sets Ethereum apart from the pack is its focus on smart contracts of all shapes and sizes. While it may seem complicated, a variation of this type of function is currently available to most checking account users in the form of automated deductions that can be set up either by the user or by a third party with the user's permission. A smart contract works in broadly the same way but from a decentralized position instead of a more centralized alternative. Put another way, a smart contract is the computer code equivalent of the legalese in a contract that stipulates how and when all the little details are carried out.

This fact, coupled with the improved ease of use of smart contracts on its platform, have lead many of the leading developers in the blockchain space to switch their apps over to the Ethereum blockchain instead. Ethereum is optimized for a much higher number of transactions per second, and the fees for each of these transactions is lower as well. What it all boils down to is that experts are already predicting that Ethereum will see as much as a ten-fold increase in popularity before the end of 2018.

Also of note is the fact that many of the applications currently under development are being developed with the focus of making the cryptocurrency process more accessible to common users and easier to understand overall. As these projects begin to come online in the next few years it is likely that they will cause usage rates to increase even more. This, in turn, makes it a strong contender to survive past the saturation point and cause its price to increase dramatically besides. Even more encouraging is the fact that major corporations including JP Morgan and Microsoft have already thrown their lot in with Ethereum by joining the Enterprise Ethereum Alliance.

Later in 2018, Ethereum is set to shake up the cryptocurrency world in a big way, with the introduction of an entirely new way of mining. The proof of stake concept eases the mining procedure where a large number of transactions need to be verified. While under the proof of work standard, a huge number of distributed miners are consistently verifying the hashes of transactions through the mining procedure so as to update the current status of the blockchain, the proof of stake idea expects clients to repeatedly demonstrate responsibility for a claim share ("stake") in the basic currency.

The hope is that the new system will improve the rate at which new blocks can be produced, which marks the first step in Buterin's continued plans for Ethereum's evolution. When the system goes wide it will mark the first time a proof of stake system has been used to secure a blockchain, which will be a major step forward, despite the modest initial rollout. It will serve as the proof of concept test for an alternate to the proof of work model that has dominated the early days of cryptocurrency development and thus provide proponents a chance to finally test their claims of its superiority. One thing that is already known for sure is the fact that when it is eventually rolled out on a larger scale the proof of stake model will reduce the amount of electricity required to verify a block significantly.

Perhaps more importantly, if you look at the transaction chart for bitcoin then you will see that it is nothing but peaks and valleys. It's true that things tend to move in an overall positive direction, but it can hardly be called steady growth. On the contrary the Ethereum chart shows a much more overall bullish outlook, even through the summer of 2017 when blockchain was at its current peak. It is important to keep in mind that cryptocurrencies are always going to be social constructs which means that Ethereum's robust network effects make it easier for the network, and its value, to continue to grow steadily moving forward. As of February 2018, one ether is worth about $800.

Wanchain: As previously mentioned, Wanchain had a successful ICO at the end of 2017. While it is not currently being traded on any exchange, it is still worth keeping an eye on as it represents the latest attempt to enable collaboration between multiple different blockchains at once. Wanchain is based on the Ethereum blockchain, with the goal of acting as a decentralized bank and allowing users to move multiple types of cryptocurrency around at once. For example, they would be able to use bitcoins to pay for a transaction on the Ethereum blockchain.

The Wanchain token, known as Wancoin is then consumed in support of these types of intra-chain or cross-chain transactions. Traditional proof-of-stake verification will be used for standard transactions which a mix of consensus and incentives will be used for cross-chain transactions.

These cross-chain connections require assets that integrate with Wanchain to be registered on the network. This is to ensure unique identification, as facilitated by secure multi-party computing and secret-sharing joint anchoring schemes to achieve minimal-cost integration through the cross-chain communication protocol without changing the original chain's implementation. Unregistered assets transferred to Wanchain can fit into custom templates, which deploy EDCCs that utilize cross-chain transaction data. As assets arrive from the origin chain, Wanchain issues corresponding equivalent tokens as a common unit of trade to use within the network. Wanchain's protocols are likely to allow more cross-platform integration for traders seeking to send value to one another by leveraging a trustless decentralized system. Wanchain is estimated to be available for trading by the summer of 2018.

Conclusion

Thank you for making it through to the end of *How to Make a Fortune Investing in ICOs and Altcoins: A Guide to Making Money from Initial Coin Offerings, and other Cryptocurrencies such as Ethereum, Litecoin, Ripple and More*, let's hope it was informative and able to provide you with all of the tools you need to achieve your goals, whatever it is that they may be. Just because you've finished this book doesn't mean there is nothing left to learn on the topic, expanding your horizons is the only way to find the mastery you seek.

When it comes to investing in cryptocurrency of any type, be it altcoin or ICO, it is important to keep in mind that the market is always changing which means reading one book and considering yourself an expert is a mistake that will cost you money in the long-run guaranteed. Rather than resting on your laurels, it is important to commit yourself to the idea of becoming a lifelong learner if you ever hope to become a cryptocurrency millionaire.

Additionally, when you are first getting started it is important to keep in mind that while some altcoins make their owners millionaires overnight, they are by far the exception, not the rule. What this means is that if you go in expecting overnight success then you are not only going to be disappointed, you are going to end up making mistakes that will take you out of the market before you ever get a chance to really get going. Remember, investing in cryptocurrency is a marathon, not a sprint, slow and steady wins the race every time.

The Complete Cryptocurrency Investor's Book Bundle

BOOK 2

Everything You Ever Wanted to Know About Bitcoin, But Were Too Afraid to Ask: All Your Questions Answered

By
Phillip J. Westbrook

© Copyright 2018-2019 - All rights reserved.

The Complete Cryptocurrency Investor's Book Bundle

"The reason why we have never found measure of wealth: we have never sought it."
--George S. Clayson, *The Richest Man in Babylon*

INTRODUCTION

Many newcomers to the cryptocurrency world consider Bitcoin to be an impenetrable enigma. Talks by computer scientists of distributed ledgers, digital hashes, Ethereum, FinTech, hard forks, and nonces leave the casual observer overwhelmed and unnecessarily confused. This book is designed to help you tackle these cryptocurrency questions so that you're left with not only an understanding of the cryptocurrency world, but also a deep appreciation of its concepts and how it works (hint: it works in the same way money does). This book will be filled with plenty of illustrations to help you understand the concepts not only in writing, but visually as well. In addition, we will explore topics such as Bitcoin mining, transactions, and security. A large component of this work—and Bitcoin in general—is how it relates to money and how it is fundamentally different from currency, as we know it.

Bitcoin may initially seem quite confusing, but similar to many concepts, once basic definitions are defined and we delve into its basic concepts, you will be much more knowledgeable about cryptocurrency.

While many 'crypto' concepts draw the (often unwanted) attention of futurists and science-savvy dilettantes, there exist many practical applications to cryptocurrency that have the potential to revolutionize various aspects of our day to day lives, including: banking, personal and financial investments, and even mortgages and home loans.

Still others with a more dollar-conscious mind may view Bitcoins—or other competing cryptocurrencies—as a potential money making machine. At the time of this writing, the value of Bitcoin has absolutely skyrocketed from being worth less than a dollar two years ago, to exceeding $10,000 per Bitcoin. This means that if you invested $1,000 in Bitcoin in 2014, you'd be a millionaire many times over by the time of this writing.

This book is designed to help the average reader learn more about Bitcoin, but will also be useful for those seeking to understand the theoretical and financial underpinnings of Bitcoin as a powerful investment tool.

How is Bitcoin Money?

Before we delve into the intricacies of Bitcoin, it is first necessary to show where this 'money' is ensconced in— cryptocurrency. This term seems to scare a lot of people (unnecessarily) because it seems foreign to our physical world of euros, dollars, yuan, and rupees. The word *crypto* stems from the Greek word 'kriptos' meaning hidden or secret. However, there is nothing secret about this hidden currency of Bitcoin (we all know about it after all).

The only difference between any cryptocurrency and paper money is that while we can touch and see paper money, cryptocurrencies are 'invisible' so to speak—they only exist online.

Initially, this seems quite scary, no? If I have a million euros in the bank, but can't see it or hold it, is it really there? Perhaps even more important, will anyone believe that I have money there? Will it be worth anything, or will it simply be considered Monopoly money? In order to answer this question, we must develop a more nuanced understanding of money and how it influences the cryptocurrency world.

So what is money? For some, it is the root of all evil. For others, such as George Bernard Shaw, *lack of* money is the root of all evil. While Shaw may be more poetically inspired, he captures an essential point—money itself is just a tool by which we sell and purchase goods. Let's take a look at the trajectory of money over the past few millennia to understand where it is going. The answers to these questions will take us through an adventure beginning in ancient history, medieval China, through credit cards, and finish with Bitcoin.

A Brief History of Money:

If we look back at the last section, we saw that money is simply a *tool* by which we conduct transactions—but this was not always the case. For millennia, our ancestors did not trade using money, but rather through a system called **barter**.

BARTER:

Let's imagine that in the village of Bedrock, Fred and Wilma Flintstone are seeking to sell some of their wool to their neighbor. Since there are no euros or marks, the only option they have is to sell their wool in return for another product, say wheat. These are the basics of the barter system—one group needs material for clothing and another needs food, so they trade their products at whatever value they consider adequate.

Astute observers may already see a problem developing here—how much wool is wheat worth? It's a bit difficult to tell, so humanity essentially eyeballed these sorts of transactions for thousands of years. Clearly, this is not the most precise of transaction systems, but at the time, it worked quite nicely. Money developed from this system because in a world where people are consistently trying to cheat each other and gain a slight edge over their neighbors,[1] a more precise unit of measurement is required.

Fred and Wilma can trade with their neighbors in their village openly and conscientiously because if they try to cheat their neighbors, their community will shun them. However, eventually people began trading with others in different communities. The Silk Route, for example, traversed dozens of countries and two continents, connecting Europe to China. We cannot expect people to act nobly when they are conducting transactions with others in a foreign land and in different languages.

GOLD:

So eventually, they developed a system where they can trade a valuable object, like a gem or gold, for their product. Now we see the development of money. In leaving the world of wool and wheat, now we enter the world of gems and gold, where they may be traded in lieu of the other products. On one hand this makes sense, gold doesn't rot, spoil, it is resilient, it's quite compact, and can be used for pretty much any transaction. However, the same problem persists: how much gold is a kilo of wheat worth? There is no objective answer to this, and if every answer is subjective, then nobody's winning. Additionally, how can someone know that the gold used in a trade is legitimate? The answer came from governments.

---

[1] It should be noted that while the modern man would immediately consider the option of extracting every bit of wool from one's neighbor for the least amount of wheat, it did not seem to occur that much to our ancestors. As proof of this, the barter system lasted for millennia. If there were extreme problems with people cheating the system to benefit themselves, this system of exchanging goods would not have lasted too long. Perhaps societal and familial pressures from others gave an impetus for people to treat each other more fairly in their transactions.

COINS

When people began congregating into larger and larger groups, they formed tribes, chiefdoms, and kingdoms. In such large communities, it became impossible to discern between real gold and counterfeits. So the chiefs, kings, pharaohs, and emperors decided to 'mark' the gold coins with their stamp of accreditation. Gold slowly became more the metal of choice because of its permanence and malleability—it could easily be engraved with the king's seal. Now that coins were authenticated with the full backing of the local government, the king was essentially ensuring their credibility. For the next millennia, and even today, coins were the preferred method of conducting transactions. However, something interesting happened in China during the 13th and 14th centuries.

PAPER CURRENCY:

Chinese merchants soon grew tired of carrying tons of heavy copper coins in their boats. These coins were so cumbersome that they not only weighed their boats down, they prevented merchants from loading their boats with more of their products.

Furthermore, should anything happen to the ship, these copper coins sunk to the bottom of the ocean, never to be recovered. To solve this problem, they developed a clever solution. Merchants in Peking, Shanghai, and Guangzhou collectively decided that they would carry pieces of marked paper[2] to represent copper coins.

When they docked in the mainland, these pieces of marked paper—also known as 'flying money' because a strong wind could send a ship's paper flying—could be traded for coins. Eventually, this system of using paper to represent more valuable products caught on, and two centuries later, the local dynastic governments began printing their names and bestowing their stamps of approval on the paper, rendering it paper currency.

TODAY:

Paper currency clearly exists to this day in the form of British pounds, dollars, rials, and pesos. The principles also remain the same. The only difference between dollars and Monopoly money is the government's stamp of approval upon the dollar bill, thereby ensuring that every subject agrees that one dollar is worth exactly that, and cannot be traded for a bill of a different value. The same concept applies to Bitcoin, and every other currency. Euros and rubles are only worth their value *because* we all agree upon it.

The moment people begin thinking that yen and rupees aren't worth anything, we'll see their values drop. As we will later explore, **Bitcoin works under the same rules**. Before we jump from paper money to Bitcoin however, we have to pass through another revolutionary new idea in the history of money: credit cards. Much of Bitcoin's success has to do with the relationship between credit cards and banks, so it is important to check out how

---

[2] At that time, China was known for pioneering a rudimentary form of paper from papyrus. Since they had papyrus to spare, paper money became the rule of the sea for Chinese merchants.

credit cards have influenced our daily lives in the 21st century

CREDIT CARDS:

When most people think of credit cards, they likely imagine American Express, MasterCard, Visa, and Discover. While all of these cards are surely considered credit cards, did you know that the precursor to these cards originated in medieval Europe? In a largely illiterate and uneducated society where most individuals could only perform basic math, a unique and clever method of keeping track of payments emerged in the form of tally sticks.

TALLY STICKS:

The concept is relatively simple: carve a few notches on a stick and split the stick in two. Let's imagine that in a Swiss canton, Mr. Cartier owes twenty francs to Mr. Baume. In order to show both parties that one owes money to another, they agree to carve twenty notches onto a tally stick. This tally stick is then cut (along the notches) so that each person has twenty half-notches on their stick. Once Mr. Cartier pays his creditor the twenty francs, the two of them put the sticks together, align up the notches, and complete the transaction.

Tally sticks additionally have a built-in counterfeiting measure. We must remember that this was a time before power tools and these sticks were broken by hand, meaning that the jagged edges of the wood would have to line up perfectly between creditor and debtor, rendering it difficult to fake a transaction or scratch off a notch. To help you understand what how tally sticks work, *Figure 1* below illustrates this rather ingenious concept.

Figure 1: Tally Sticks[3]

Tally sticks had unique notches, and then split lengthwise so the two halves matched perfectly and could not be counterfeited or changed.

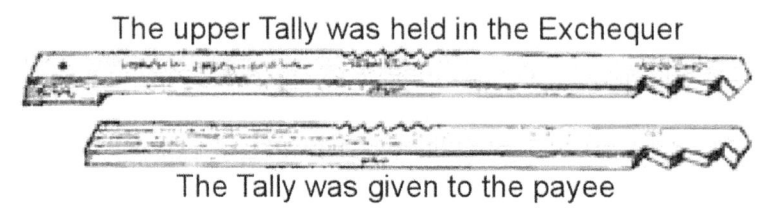

The upper Tally was held in the Exchequer

The Tally was given to the payee

This method of payment existed in Medieval Europe for centuries and it was not abolished until 1826 in England. Not long after the abolition of tally sticks[4] did credit cards become 'the name of the game' for many consumers.

E-COMMERCE:

Unlike tally sticks, credit cards skyrocketed the transaction world into cyberspace, with most transactions occurring between credit cards and businesses. Also differing from tally sticks is that credit cards can charge interest—a concept that was eschewed and considered usury under canon law during the Middle Ages in Europe.

---

[3] Photo taken from The Ben Williams Library, found at http://benwilliamslibrary.com/blog/wp-content/uploads/2015/04/th.jpg

[4] The British even used them for taxation purposes before they were abolished!

SUMMARY:

Something interesting is happening here, no? Let's briefly recount this 'ascent of money'[5] from the beginning of time to the present:

- At one time money didn't exist, as the general system of trading was barter.

- Then money went from being the product itself to becoming precious gemstones and gold.

- Over time, gold became the preferred method of transactions, mostly because leaders could engrave their names and profiles onto the gold coins. While this was revolutionary enough, the gold itself still had a (largely symbolic) value. Gold itself cannot clothe or feed a person, but it's what it can buy that matters. As evidence of this, for example, *the Inca people could not comprehend how the Spanish were willing to kill every last one of them to extract what they considered to be a relatively useless yellow metal in the ground.*

- The transition to gold was impressive, but when that became cumbersome, the Chinese developed paper money, which rules to this day.

---

[5] I credit this term to Niall Ferguson, who named his *magnum opus* 'The Ascent of Money.'

- Meanwhile in Europe, tally sticks allow people to borrow and loan money accurately, becoming the precursor to credit cards.

- Money has transferred from gems, to gold, to paper, to cards, to now with Bitcoin, disappearing altogether.

How Does Bitcoin Play Into this Trajectory in the World of Money?

So how does Bitcoin fit into the monetary world?

What exactly is so different about cryptocurrencies that alters the trajectory of money itself?

Well as we can see throughout the history of money, the value of money has become more and more subjective. Fred Flintstone knew exactly how much food he needed for the day, and was able to trade his wool for the day's wheat. Yet gold, although valuable enough, cannot be eaten. It needs to be traded for food.

The same logic holds for paper money; its worthless in and of itself and quite cheap to produce. For example, the US Mint spends more or less the same amount on the production of a five-dollar bill than a one hundred-dollar bill. The important thing to note is that the Mint *spends* money on *producing* money.

This aspect is quite counterintuitive to the currency world. This is also partially why gold went out of fashion—it had to be mined. During the Great Recession years, an interesting concept emerged from the shadows of plummeting stocks—what if we can create a currency that was free to produce and could only be generated through work? Here is where Bitcoin jumps into the currency world.

A Brief History of Bitcoin:

SHADOWY BEGINNINGS:

In 2008, an anonymous computer scientist by the name of Satoshi Nakamoto developed what we now call Bitcoin. Legends, rumors, and conspiracy theories abound about who exactly is Satoshi Nakamoto. Truth is, we have little to go on when it comes to Satoshi—and this may be a pseudonym for another person or group of people. Judging from the name, one would initially be led to believe that this person is a Japanese man. However, there have several audio clips with this individual and all accounts indicate an American man, without the slightest hint of a Japanese accent.

While evidence such as this lends itself to irregularities and suspicions regarding the true nature of Satoshi, others have hypothesized that Satoshi Nakamoto is a *nom de guerre* for a group of computer scientists and that Bitcoin is a more collective endeavor rather than the brainchild of any single individual.

These rumors may be the most off-putting aspect of Bitcoin for future investors, buyers, and consumers. If we don't know who is really behind Bitcoin, and if they have gone to these lengths to hide themselves, do they have sinister motives? People continue to speculate about these questions and there still don't seem to be any decisive answers. However, let's leave the world of cloaks and daggers and enter cyberspace. Rumors and speculation aside, Bitcoin solves many problems that currently exist with currency.

How is Bitcoin Different than paper currency?

THE INTERNET NECESSITY:

Unlike paper currency, Bitcoin operates solely in the world of computers, and in order to access Bitcoin, you must have Internet. As many reading this book can already surmise, right off the bat, Bitcoin helps one group over another. Predictably, new advances also benefit the richer 'Global North' over the generally poorer 'Global South.' Helene in Denmark may have easy access to Internet in Copenhagen. She may be able to walk from her home to any café and never lose Internet connection. Unfortunately, Daoud in Djibouti may have a tougher time gaining access to Internet, which may only be found in the town center and be prohibitively expensive.

It is true that Bitcoin is free to create (gold has to be mined and paper money must be printed), but if Bitcoin has any cost, it is the unrecovered cost of an Internet connection. Clearly the main difference between Bitcoin and any other physical currency is that while Internet connection does cost money, it can be used for almost anything and not just conducting financial transactions.

We have purposefully informed you of Bitcoin's main drawbacks first, so that we can end this introduction on a positive note.

UNIVERSAL ACCEPTANCE:

Unlike physical currency that is limited to the national level (e.g., Canadian dollars are only valid in Canada, and not in New Zealand), one of the main benefits of Bitcoin is that, since it's an Internet-based currency, it is universally accepted.

Essentially, if Sandra in Spain wants to send some money to her friend, Alex, in Australia, she can do so with Bitcoin cognizant that this cryptocurrency is equally valid in Madrid as it is in Melbourne. In this sense, Bitcoin is the first truly international and universal currency[6] that transcends borders, cultures, and languages.

While the euro may come in second, no physical currency can compete with Bitcoin's universality. Again, its transcendence of borders is valid, but this only exists if the user has access to Internet. Because of this, access to Bitcoin is more limited in what scholars call 'developing countries.'

INFLATION PROTECTION:

Ironically enough, the people that Bitcoin is poised to help most are those who are least likely to benefit from this new currency. Let me explain. Bitcoin is not subject to the same inflationary tendencies that physical currencies are susceptible to.

For those economically minded readers, **inflation** occurs when a country attempts to improve the living conditions of its subjects by printing money. These practices do not, in reality, improve anyone's living conditions; in fact, they make them worse. Because producers know that everyone has more money in their pockets, they feel comfortable charging more for their products.

The United States, for example, has experienced a constant (and controlled) inflation of 3% over the past thirty years. It is because of this that we hear of a full meal costing 50 cents back in

---

[6] This statement, of course, must be footnoted with some talk of other attempted-international currencies. During the years of Pan-Arabism, some Middle East states decided to join together to form one state—notably Syria, Iraq, and Egypt—meaning that they would have shared a currency. Similarly, and more importantly, the Euro has been adopted by dozens of states in Europe. The difference between these cases and Bitcoin is that the latter is completely transnational in that it is not bounded by geography, culture, or foreign boundaries.

the 1970s.

Inflation may not be much of a problem in a developed country like the United States, but it's more problematic in a place like Zimbabwe, which reached a record 79 billion percent in 2008! This means that if someone had 79 billion Zimbabwean dollars in 2016, it would be worth one Zimbabwean dollar today. How can anyone ever save money in these types of situations?

Well, Bitcoin may offer an answer: If private citizens in Zimbabwe decide to invest their money in Bitcoin and conduct transactions using this cryptocurrency, then they would be able to **hedge** (to use the financial term) against the Zimbabwean dollar.[7] The only way for Zimbabweans to conduct transactions using Bitcoin, however, is for them to have access to Internet. That said, even though many in developing countries have trouble accessing Internet, this technology is spreading to more and more people each day.

Bitcoin has the potential to undermine all of the physical currencies that we have touched upon. Furthermore, the banking and credit card industries can greatly benefit from Bitcoin's peer to peer (P2P) transactions. All of these topics will be discussed in great detail in the next few chapters. First however, it is necessary to go through some technical terms relating to Bitcoin, cryptocurrencies, and blockchain technology. If you are already somewhat familiar with Bitcoin, feel free to skip this chapter, otherwise read on.

---

[7] In reality, many fiscally minded citizens of the developing world save their money in US dollars, British pounds, or euros, knowing that these currencies are more stable and less susceptible to inflationary practices in their home countries. This has become such a common practice that in countries like Venezuela, where the bolivar is decreasing in value every day, many citizens are refusing to conduct business in the local currency, preferring dollars instead.

CHAPTER 2: CRYPTOCURRENCY LINGO

Computer scientists and cryptocurrency fanatics love to speak in complex technical terms that not only ensure that an esoteric audience is listening, it also makes them seem smart. Because of this, many people are afraid to delve deeper into Bitcoin. This chapter is designed to help you navigate through the oftentimes-confusing language surrounding Bitcoin.

In addition, we are including a glossary of very-much needed terms so that if the reader forgets any of these concepts, they can easily find them at the end of this work. First and foremost, as we have already noticed, cryptocurrencies are money that exists only online. The most famous of these currencies, of course, is Bitcoin. But how does Bitcoin work? The answer lies is blockchain technology.

THE BLOCKCHAIN:

This technology holds the core of Bitcoin's success together, so it's important to dive deeper into this meaning. However, the concept of the blockchain is rather complex and can be a bit cumbersome to explain. If you are merely looking to invest in Bitcoin, rest assured that you do not need to know every last detail of this chapter.

This section is mostly for those who are interested in understanding the foundational computer science principles in the bedrock of Bitcoin. For the casual investor and learner, very little of this comes into play and you will unlikely ever hear of this part of Bitcoin.

That said, it is still beneficial to have an understanding of how Bitcoin, by adopting blockchain technology, works. Understanding the blockchain will also give you a leg up on other Crypto novices and help you to make better financial decisions when it comes to investing and trading Bitcoin.

Blockchain technology, as the name suggests, is composed of both blocks and chains of data. But what does this mean? Surely it doesn't mean physical blocks and chains? Naturally, in cyberspace, blockchain technology refers to the system used by Bitcoin to conduct transactions. While there are blocks and chains in the computer, they are not physical. An illustration is in order. Below in *Figure 2* you will find an example of a computer blockchain separated into the components of each block and chain.

Figure 2: Blockchain Technology (Source: NextSpace)[8]

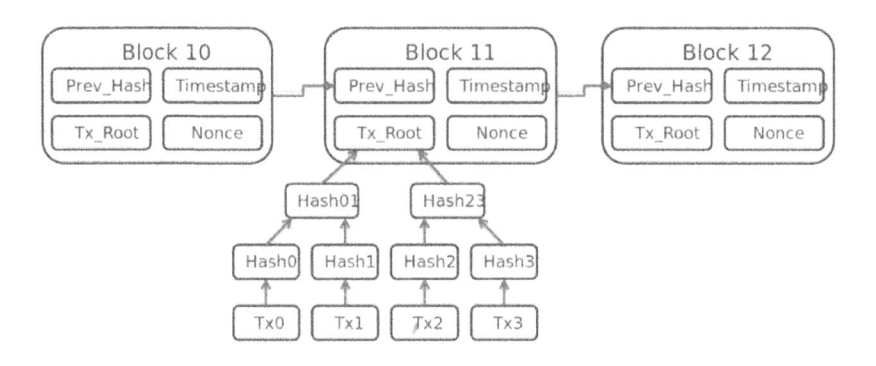

The diagram in *Figure 2* illustrates a traditional blockchain. As you can see, each block is composed of four different components: a previous hash, a root hash (shown in the image as **Tx_root**, and also known as '**Merkle Root**' and '**Merkle Hash**'), a **timestamp**, and a **nonce**. Before we examine and define each of these terms, let's first examine the linkages between these blocks.

As most have predicted, they are called chains, connecting one block to its neighbor. Each chain connects one block to another, meaning that if you trace one blockchain all the way back, you'll find the first block in the chain. The chains are easy to explain, but now let's look into each block and see what they're all made up of.

---

[8] This image can be found at https://thenextspace.co/education/technology/blockchain-bitcoin-cryptotoken-masterclass/

BLOCKS:

Each block is made up of two different hashes: a previous hash and a root hash. But what in the world is a 'hash?' To many, hash is slang for a type of drug. Not so for Satoshi Nakamoto.

HASHES:

Hashes are bits of encrypted code 20 digits long (I.E., 0F23J3NOGB7WM314YWJD). These 20-digit hashes are difficult to reproduce and counterfeit because of the nearly infinite number of combinations available for each encrypted code. So let's look at each hash. First is the **previous hash**, which is probably the most complicated of all of the components (but really not too complicated).

The **previous hash** in *Figure 2* is a piece of code depicting where the block came from. This encrypted code not only informs us of the block's history by consisting of parts of the previous block. These components of its predecessor are depicted in *Figure 2* as Hash01 and Hash23. Meanwhile, each of these hashes are composed of two other hashes, Hash0 and Hash1, combine to form Hash01, and Hash2 and Hash3 compose Hash23. Each of these hashes also have their own previous hashes, and so on *ad infinitum*.

What's the Point of the Hashes?

Because of these previous hashes, we can know where each block has been. Imagine if Jenny has a $10 bill. She may know that she received this particular $10 as change for her shopping in Chicago. However, before this 10-dollar bill was in the cash register, Jenny has no idea where it was. It could have belonged to her neighbor, a wealthy billionaire, a counterfeiter, or a criminal.

With blockchain technology's previous hash, she could know exactly which account her money has passed through. Whereas in the physical world, we are only separated by one transaction, in blockchain, we can trace back the origins of each block (and therefore, Bitcoin) to its creation with the previous hash. Let's suppose that someone was bent on doing exactly this. They could trace previous hash to previous hash for a long time, or they could skip all of that and go directly to the **root hash**.

The **root hash**, or Merkle root/hash, shows the origins of any specific block and also serves a sort of ID card for the block. With this identification, the user can know that the block was created. Once a block is created, it cannot disappear. This creates an extra level of security because it doesn't necessarily allow Bitcoins to be laundered in the same way a drug trafficker can launder dollar bills. The root hash depicts the creation of the block and the previous hash shows where that block has been. What drug criminal would conduct transactions using these conditions?

The truth is very few because even though Pablo Escobar may want the big bucks, (aka Bitcoin), the blockchain technology ensures that there is always a paper trail. (This is also why drug dealers always deal in cash and never accept credit cards or checks for their illicit activities, but let's not digress). Back in the (legal) Bitcoin world, root hashes serve a necessary security function, but there are two more parts to each block.

TIMESTAMP:

The **timestamp** is probably the easiest part of the block to comprehend.

It simply shows when a new block was created. Not only does this timestamp authenticate the existence of the block, it also *cannot be altered in any way*. Furthermore, because the timestamp cannot be removed, there is an extra level of security built into the block within its existence in cyberspace. The timestamp allows anybody in the network to track the existence of any single block, making it effectively impossible to not leave a paper trail.

NONCE:

The final component of the block is the **nonce**. As a side note, many user accounts, Bitcoin aficionados, blockchain enthusiasts, and cryptocurrency buffs love to incorporate the word 'nonce' into their usernames, blogs, and even vernacular. Even though the name sounds weird, don't be alarmed; the concept is quite simple.

The nonce is simply a randomly generated number. When a human thinks of a randomly generated number, they may come up with 7 or 14. However, these numbers are easy to predict (and replicate). On the other hand, the nonces in blockchain technology are digits as high as 2^{31}, meaning that it is nearly impossible for a human to replicate this number.

The nonce, combined with the timestamp, root hash, and previous hash (which is itself composed of all the previous blocks), makes blockchain technology quite difficult to compromise, even with a super computer. However, there is one final aspect of blockchain technology, which is adopted by Bitcoin, which adds an almost impenetrable layer of security—the **distributed ledger**.

THE DISTRIBUTED LEDGER:

Another useful term to understand the basics of Bitcoin is the concept of a distributed ledger. Before we delve into what a *distributed ledger* is, we must first understand what a ledger is. Any reader familiar with accounting knows that the accountant keeps track of all financial documentation and transactions in what is called a **ledger**.

This **ledger** is a method of book-keeping at the heart of economic transactions, but more specifically, an accountant's ledger is a **centralized ledger**, because all of the information is stored in one location.

Let's imagine that Mr. Contador in Seville is the accountant for a small business. The firm needs to buy supplies and sell finished products just like any store. Mr. Contador's ledger would show incoming revenues along with expenses. Hopefully, if the business is doing well there will be more revenue that expenses, but the only way for Mr. Contador to know that is to track all of the transactions for the fiscal year. This is an example of a ledger, but more specifically, it's a **centralized ledger**.

All of the economic transactions are accounted for in one place, specifically Mr. Contador's ledger. Over the past few decades, modern-day companies have expanded this notion of the centralized ledger to not only include supercomputers, but also to conduct a whole host of transactions, ranging from email and calendar invites, to the traditional fiscal dealings.

For many years, centralized ledgers worked very well, as they contain accounts for recording transactions in one, safe location. However, over time, computer hackers realized that if they wanted to breach the security system of a large corporation, they would simply have to hack into one computer. This is a difficult feat, to be sure, but still possible.

Take a look at the security breaches into Yahoo's email accounts over the past year, and you'll see the potential dangers of a centralized ledger. A security breach to these computers is akin to somebody breaking into Mr. Contador's small business and stealing his ledger. Yet when this happens to a large corporation containing, such as Yahoo, millions of email usernames, passwords, and otherwise private information is compromised.

As is typical with computers, a security breach is not just the theft of a single email or password; it is a large-scale, systemic threat to the system that compromises all accounts and passwords, not just one. In order to combat this potentially disastrous scenario, Bitcoin adopts the concept of a **distributed ledger**. It's perhaps easier to visually observe the difference between a **centralized**, **decentralized**, and **distributed ledger** in the figure below.

Figure 3: Different Types of Ledgers (Source: Grissom 2017)[9]

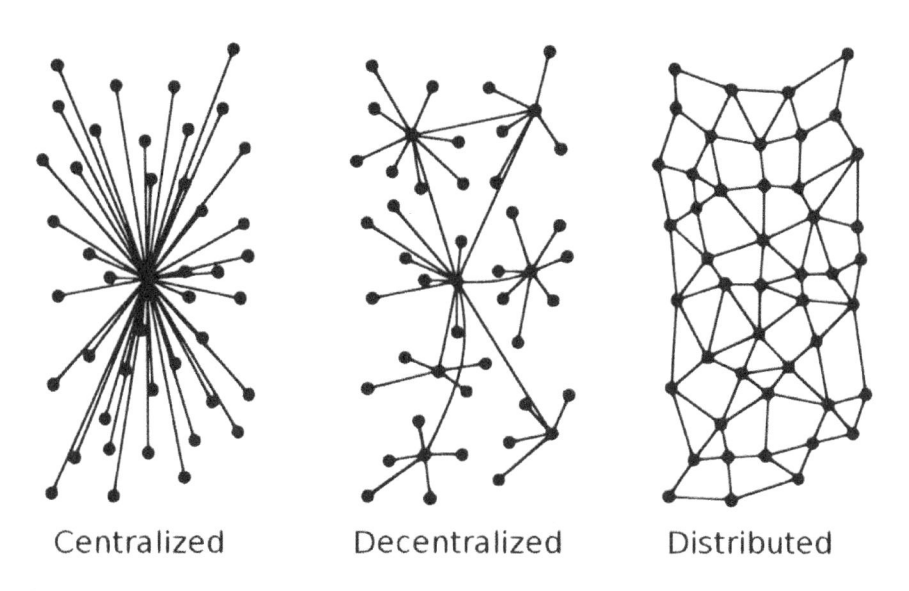

Centralized   Decentralized   Distributed

The centralized ledger works in the same way Mr. Contador's paper ledger worked. It held the information of all transactions in one centralized location (for Mr. Contador it was in his accounting book; for a multinational corporation it's in supercomputers).

A **decentralized ledger** conducts the same procedure on a

---

[9] *Figure 3* is taken from Grissom's blog at https://steemit.com/crypto/@jfgrissom/who-controls-crypto-currencies

smaller scale. This is considered somewhat safer than a centralized ledger because if a hacker attacks a supercomputer (shown as a node in the decentralized model), then only the accounts connected to that node get jeopardized. On the other hand, we see what a distributed ledger looks like in the right side of *Figure 3*.

In a **distributed ledger**, such as the one used by Bitcoin in its blockchain, when a file (called a block) gets saved, it does not only get saved onto the user's computer. It gets saved onto every single computer in the network. Suppose that Ahmad in Cairo wants to save a paper he's writing in a safe location online.

EXAMPLE:
- CENTRALIZED: If he saves his essay onto his laptop, this would be an example of a centralized ledger. If someone were interested in stealing Ahmad's paper, they would have to break into his laptop to retrieve the information.

- DISTRIBUTED: However, let's imagine that Ahmad thinks his paper has the potential to revolutionize his industry and wants to keep his information as safe as possible. He could choose to save his work onto a distributed ledger in a blockchain. This would encrypt the data so that only he can access it and then save his essay onto every single computer in the blockchain network.

This means that if someone were to hack the system, they would be forced to break into each computer in the network, which potentially could be millions of users, at the same time and alter the information identically across all of the computers.

While I hesitate to call a distributed ledger unbreakable, nothing is impossible. However, as far as security goes, distributed ledgers are by far more secure than centralized and decentralized ledgers.

Again, if you are the casual investor in Bitcoin, much of this information is not absolutely vital to your goals to your goals, and if it doesn't make much sense to you, don't sweat it. However, if you are interested in learning the intricacies of Bitcoin and investing more in cryptocurrencies in general, this may be useful information to know before you bet your money on Bitcoin. In learning these concepts you'll know "enough to be dangerous" as they say. And you'll be able to hold your own in any Bitcoin discussion.

Summary:

Let's quickly review what we have learned about Bitcoin:

THE BAD:

- First, the bad news: yes, Bitcoin's founder(s) is an anonymous person, and it is understood that this does not bode well for those looking to invest in this cryptocurrency as it is difficult to trust Satoshi Nakamoto, if that is indeed this person's name.

- It is additionally suggestive that if this anonymous person speaks with an American accent, why is his name Japanese? Legends and folk tales may lend credence to Bitcoin's mystique, but it provides little comfort for future investors that may be more interested in a profit and a secure investment.

- The next downside regarding Bitcoin is that it is only available to those with Internet. This drawback should not deter future investors—especially since access to Internet is growing exponentially—but it should be noted that the people who are best positioned to gain from Bitcoin are precisely those who cannot have access to it because Internet is either unavailable or else prohibitively expensive.

THE GOOD:

- Now that the bad news is out of the way, we can focus on how Bitcoin can be a force for progress in the investment and banking industry. We saw how the Zimbabwean person can now hedge against their currency by conducting transactions in Bitcoin and how it may be used to bet against inflation.
- Bitcoin is a cryptocurrency that works by using blockchain technology along a distributed ledger. As we saw, blockchain technology is composed of—as the name insinuates—blocks and chains. The chains are easy enough to understand, but the blocks are a bit more complex and are composed of the following: root hash, previous hash, timestamp, and nonce.
- All of these blocks and chains are then saved onto a distributed ledger, which records transactions onto every single computer in the network—a figure that can reach millions of users.

You now have the basic tools to understand the history and building blocks of Bitcoin. In the next section, we are going to examine the finer points of Bitcoin (e.g., security, mining, etc.), how it relates to our lives, and how it potentially revolutionizes banking and investment.

CHAPTER 3: YOUR BITCOIN QUESTIONS ANSWERED

In this section, we are going to tackle the most pressing questions revolving around Bitcoin and cryptocurrencies. Each question will be marked in **bold**, with the answer succeeding it. There may be many different types of readers here: potential investors, Bitcoin miners, cryptocurrency enthusiasts, casual learners, and possible users of Bitcoin. Because of the variety of readers, we are splitting up the questions into broad categories so that you can skip to the question that is most pertinent to you. The first question may interest the general public:

What is the obsession with Bitcoin?

Bitcoin has had an incredible trajectory over the past few years, skyrocketing from worth nearly nothing to over $10,000 in the second half of 2017. What started off as a sort of computer experiment has turned out to be a great success! But what happened here?

In the long term, there has been a general tendency to cross country frontiers in the world market. Large-scale advances, such as the trend of globalization and financialization that took the world by storm in the post-Cold War Era traversed many nation-state lines. People are much more comfortable in dealing with business negotiations in other countries than ever before! Because of this, the 'marketplace' was something that used to exist on the local level.

With the advent of the Internet, cross country jets, and computer technology, now the 'marketplace' exists worldwide. Bitcoin is just another component of this expansion and globalization. Keep in mind that in 2002, dozens of European states decided to forfeit their national currencies, be it the franc, the mark, the peso, or the lira, in favor of a collective currency—the euro. This was unprecedented! Fifty years ago, nobody would have thought that these countries, which had fought against each other in two world wars, would combine forces to create a united currency.

Yet here we are in 2017, not only with the euro, but also with Bitcoin—the world's first truly universal currency.

So why the obsession? Well Bitcoin is a revolutionary new idea, bedrocked on pre-existing notions. Remember how we spoke about how money has gone from gold, to paper, to cards, to disappearing altogether? Bitcoin is the embodiment of that last part of money. Because it cannot be physically held, its value is only what other people say it is. This may be fickle though because in the same way that the price of Bitcoin can skyrocket, it can just as easily plummet. Now that we have the bad news out of the way, let's move on to the good news.

IT'S A REVOLUTION:

Bitcoin can quite possibly revolutionize the banking and investment industry.

Picture this scenario:

Hans in Berlin owes his landlord his monthly rent that is due at the first of the month. His landlord, Gabrielle, is insistent that he pays his due on time.

However, Hans got paid from his job on the 30th and needs to take the money out of his bank account. It takes the bank three to five business days to process the money transfer from his job, and then takes a bit more for them to process Hans' withdrawal. Before you know it, a week passes, and Hans still has not paid Gabrielle. If this transaction were done with Bitcoin, Hans would have little trouble, as money can be passed from one person to another (called peer-to-peer transactions, or P2P) instantaneously. With Bitcoin, by adopting blockchain technology, when Hans gets paid, he can immediately transfer the money to Gabrielle without having to incur the penalties of paying his rent late.

This concept can be applied to almost any other industry. Imagine instantaneous investment banking or receiving money instantly from a friend instead of waiting the usual three to five business days.

In addition to the practical benefits to using Bitcoin in our daily lives, there exists a certain **mystique** regarding cryptocurrencies. Satoshi Nakamoto's enigmatic presence aside, Bitcoin seems to come at us from the future, and the stock market proves this. Before we delve into the concept of investing in Bitcoin (we will ask this question later), let's first see what problems Bitcoin solves. We have alluded to many of them throughout these sections, but there are tangible benefits regarding Bitcoin that we should explore.

What problems does Bitcoin solve?

FLAWS IN OUR CURRENT SYSTEM:

There exist a few problems with our current system of money. First of all, it costs money to make money. This in itself seems ludicrous. Take a look at these statistics: it costs the US Mint 4.9 cents to make a $1 bill and 10.9 cents to make a $5 bill. One would think that the price per unit would continue going up for larger bills due to the extra security measures that the Mint imprints onto every dollar, but this is not so! Amazingly enough, it costs the US Mint 10.3 cents to make a $10 bill and 10.5 cents to make $20 and $50 bills. Why the price of a $5 bill is more expensive than a $10, $20, or $50 bill is beyond the scope of this work (though perhaps economies of scale come into play here – but that is just speculation).

Naturally, given the large security measures, such as watermarks and magnetic strips, put in place into the $100 bill, a Benjamin costs 12.3 cents. The marginal gains from minting coins are almost not worth the hassle, with the cost of making one penny hovering at around 1.7 cents and nickels cost around 8 cents.[10] This means that the government actually loses money in order to produce money.

SAVING MONEY ON PRODUCING MONEY:

At one time, printing money was a way of ensuring that businesses and consumers could conduct transactions. With the end of the gold standard and the floating dollar, it has become less and less important to print money, as many transactions are already conducted online and without the physical transfer of cash.

While you may not know it, most of your money already exists in cyberspace in the form of digital numbers on your telephone or computer screen. If banks, investment companies, Fortune 500 conglomerates, and small businesses began using Bitcoin as a standard currency, it would save governments (and therefore, taxpayers) the hassle of creating their own currencies.

OBLITERATING EXCHANGE RATES

Along this train of thought, have you ever passed by money

---

[10] This information is largely taken from CNN Money, found here: http://money.cnn.com/2016/01/11/news/economy/u-s-coins/index.html

exchange kiosks in the airport? Let's say Dimitrios in Athens travels to Johannesburg. He would have to exchange his euro for the South African Rand at the airport (and get ripped off with the exchange rates in the process). Bitcoin would effectively render this industry obsolete. Because it is universally accepted as a cryptocurrency, Bitcoin would work just as well in Greece as in South Africa.

However, just because that industry would be altered, doesn't mean that it will go away forever. Bitcoin is simply a strong competition for those physical currency exchanges. If they were smart, they would slowly adopt Bitcoin (and other cryptocurrencies) into their system of money exchange.

BENEFITTING THE MANY DESPITE CURRENCY SITUATIONS:

When a player like Bitcoin revolutionizes an industry, we must always ask ourselves, *cui bono*, who benefits? Well, if we were to answer honestly, it seems like those who invested in Bitcoin from the outset benefit most. That said, Bitcoin could always benefit more and more people, especially if the physical currencies around them are burning to the ground (e.g., the Zimbabwean dollar). However, we must also ask ourselves the opposite—who loses? Bitcoin has solved one problem, but may have created many enemies. If a cryptocurrency developed by an anonymous computer scientist can compete with the mighty dollar, euro, British pound, ruble, and yuan, then Bitcoin has managed to unite every single government against them. If there is any industry that governments hold a monopoly over, it's the currency making industry!

THE DESTRUCTION OF CURRENCY:

Up until Bitcoin, only governments have had the political fiat to print money for their constituencies. If Bitcoin undermines that power, then it has found something that all governments can agree upon. How nations will react to the ascent of Bitcoin still is in the speculative stage, but if Bitcoin poses a true threat to all fiat currencies, then the collective government response worldwide would be strong. While this scenario is unlikely, Bitcoin solves the problem that many travellers have had over the years; you lose money because you are exchanging money through a middleman. With Bitcoin, since you won't have to exchange money, there will be no middleman. Let's take a look at how else middlemen are sidelined with Bitcoin.

As we alluded previously, Bitcoin is also a valuable tool for speeding up P2P money exchanges. But that's not all. Because Bitcoin implements a distributed ledger to keep track of all money transfers, the system is much safer than if your friend gave you a $20 bill or if they electronically wired the same amount to your bank account.

Your encrypted information spread out over the entire network would be nearly impossible to jeopardize. Furthermore, precisely because Bitcoin is capable of conducting these P2P money transfers automatically, it does not need the fables (and hated) middleman.

WHAT BANKS ARE ACTUALLY DOING WITH YOUR MONEY:

The real reason why banks, investment institutions, and financial corporations take three to five business days to conduct even the simplest of transactions is because they have armies of accountants, clerks, and managers ensuring that the money goes from 'Point A' to 'Point B' correctly.

Also, and even moreso, it's because they're using your money for other banking functions and therefore they need to acquire the money back from somewhere to make a payment on your behalf. If you deposit money in your account, the bank will be using that money to lend to others and to fulfill loans while you may be under the delusion that your money is just sitting there.

Due to its distributed ledger, which effectively keeps an eye out over the entire system, Bitcoin transactions do not require this sort of manpower, and your money is readily available to you. If there is any problem that Bitcoin solves, it is that it automates currency exchanges. Bitcoin has effectively brought currencies into the 21st century by automating transactions that previously were laborious and costly.

Remember Hans and his landlord Gabrielle? The only reason it took Hans three to five business days to extract his money from the bank was because he had to wait for all of the middlemen in his bank to process his request. This not only takes time, it also costs the bank a lot of money because they have to pay all of these employees. It's no wonder that Fortune 500 companies are looking to **blockchain** technology (and by extension, Bitcoin) to streamline their accounting processes.

Bitcoin solves many important problems, and the ones listed above are just a few of them, but as we saw, it creates a few more. This begs the question, however, what is the point? Why should I use Bitcoin rather than fiat currency that works relatively well for my limited needs?

In the next section we are going to discover the ways in which you could use Bitcoin in your daily lives. You may realize that this is hardly different than how you would conduct day-to-day transactions using USD, Euros, Dinars and Rand.

How can we use Bitcoin?

INCREASING POPULARITY:

You may be surprised to find out that you can pay for online dating websites and the computer you're using to boot using Bitcoin! Due to its astronomic increase in popularity, Bitcoin is starting to be accepted by many corporations, online marketplaces, and even non-profits.[11] While it may not come as a surprise that companies, such as mint.com, which is a financial planning website, accepts Bitcoin, other companies, such as Microsoft, are getting in on the action.

Furthermore, you can donate to Save the Children or Wikipedia if you are so inclined, with Bitcoin. But the fun doesn't end there; Overstock has partnered with Coinbase to become the first major retailer to accept this cryptocurrency. Virgin Galactic and Peach Airlines have also thrown their hat into the ring. You can even use Bitcoin to buy a Tesla, and yes, OkCupid does accept Bitcoin.

Computer apps, such as Shopify and Square are also Bitcoin compatible. Finally, lest we get too anecdotal, you can even buy

---

[11] The following information is taken from https://steemit.com/bitcoin/@steemitguide/2017-top-list-of-big-companies-that-accept-bitcoin-and-cryptocurrencies

(some) food with Bitcoin, with Subway[12] and Magnificent Tea accepting this cryptocurrency.

Bitcoin has a long way to go before it can compete with the usability and ubiquity of the dollar, but the companies named above are not small or fringe corporations (well, Virgin Galactic comes close). Rather, they are respected and large corporations. More importantly, they are not just computer-based companies, but rather automotive (Tesla), encyclopedic (Wikipedia), restaurants and food (Subway), and consumer-based (Overstock).

What is most impressive is the sheer variety of all of these companies that have little to do with each other. Virgin Galactic and OkCupid have little in common other than the fact that they both accept payment through Bitcoin.

What is even more impressive is that the majority of the corporations named above have only recently begun accepting Bitcoin as payment. It seems like we are still in the growing phase of Bitcoin acceptance and that this trajectory has not plateaued over time. There are some exceptions. For example, Expedia, the online travel conglomerate, has accepted Bitcoin as payment since 2014. Similarly to Overstock, they are aligning themselves with Coinbase to accept this cryptocurrency.

Perhaps on a more worrying note, many computer hackers are hacking government databases, which, as you may have guessed, use centralized ledgers rather than the distributed ledgers of blockchain, and demand payment in Bitcoin! While these cases remain anecdotal, it is impressive that Bitcoin is considered a viable medium of exchange among criminals as well.

---

[12] Subway's stance on accepting Bitcoin can be found at https://99bitcoins.com/who-accepts-bitcoins-payment-companies-stores-take-bitcoins/

Why Doesn't Every Merchant Accept Bitcoin?

Yet, as always, we must ask ourselves why aren't more companies accepting Bitcoin as payment? Online investment information coming from the Motley Fool has a few suggestions. First, Bitcoin remains "exceptionally volatile, and even overnight settlements could result in businesses losing out on a lot of money."
They continue, stating that "Bitcoin prices plunged by more than $200 in a single day between June 25 and June 26. Businesses that had conducted transactions in Bitcoin with next-day settlement could have seen between 7% and 10% of their deal value depleted in a matter of hours (Williams 2017).[13] They have a point, but we will discuss investing in Bitcoin a bit later.

The other reason why other companies are not investing in Bitcoin was already alluded to but needs a different slant: Bitcoin can become so popular that it may incur the ire of governmental regulators.
 If Bitcoin begins "acting as a bridge currency for marijuana purchases looks like the perfect reason for U.S. lawmakers to consider imposing regulations on the cryptocurrency. As long as the government leaves bitcoin alone, it has an opportunity to thrive" (Ibid.). But let's be real—most governments may not allow Bitcoin to fully thrive without creating a system of checks and balances to hinder its progression.

The next question that we answer is quite possibly the most itching question that readers have, and accordingly, it will be the question with the longest response: how do we make money off Bitcoin? Because there are many ways to make money off Bitcoin, it is perhaps best to split up the question into two sections, which

---

[13] Information taken from Sean William's article from July 6, 2017 found at https://www.fool.com/investing/2017/07/06/5-brand-name-businesses-that-currently-accept-bite.aspx

will be explained in greater detail below: mining and investing.

How do I make money off Bitcoin?

Isn't this the million-dollar (or Bitcoin, if you're so inclined) question? As mentioned in the previous section, there are two main ways to capitalize upon Bitcoin's success—**mining** and **investing**.

In keeping with the style of the book, let's start off with the more difficult topic of mining before we delve into the aspect of investing, which is admittedly more exciting. If you are interested in learning about the internal makings of Bitcoin, then this section ought to interest you, as it answers many mysteries surrounding Bitcoin. We know how fiat currency is made—it is minted at a government agency. However, how exactly are Bitcoin released into circulation?

BITCOIN MINING:

The method that most governments use to print paper money is much more cost effective than previous strategies. The Spanish, for example, nearly bankrupted themselves trying to find more and more gold in America. By those standards, the twelve cents it takes the US Mint to make a $100 Benjamin is quite efficient.

However, if we are to take currency (along with everything that comes with it) into the 21st century, then we would have to regenerate it for free. This is, more or less, how Bitcoin mining works. Clearly, when we are talking of **Bitcoin mining**, this does not refer to actual digging for gold—those days are long gone. In Bitcoin mining, users solve mathematical problems to gain more Bitcoin.

That last statement clearly deserves a more nuanced answer. Let's say that Venkat in Calcutta is interested in mining for Bitcoin. He can begin doing so by physically solving a math problem for Bitcoin. Usually, in the beginning, it's something simple, like 517 minus 314. As Venkat solves more and more math problems, they become more and more difficult. In return for Venkat's work solving math problems, he is rewarded with Bitcoins.

This essentially incentivizes him into solving more complex algorithms. However, soon Venkat is going to have a problem: there will come a time when he either cannot solve a math problem, or it will take too long for him to solve one. Essentially, the number of Bitcoin returned to Venkat for solving math problems (mining) is not worth the time he spent working on math problems.

So what can he do to solve this dilemma? He can subcontract friends to do the work for him, but that requires paying him off. If Venkat is astute, he'll create a computer program on his laptop to begin solving math problems at a faster rate than he can do so with pen and paper.

USING COMPUTERS:

Suppose that Venkat did this: he ditched his pen and paper and his computer began conducting math problems for him. In return for his computer's labor, Venkat received Bitcoin. In the early days of Bitcoin, this was quite a possibility. However, times have changed. Pretty soon, Venkat's computer processor could not cope with the volume of others also mining for Bitcoin by solving these algorithmic problems.

USING COMPUTER "STEROIDS"

Pretty soon, others discovered that if they insert computer graphic cards into their computers, they could mine for Bitcoin at a faster rate than simply using a computer processor. So Venkat goes to his local store and buys some of these graphic cards and inserts them into his computer to continue mining for Bitcoin. This works relatively well until his electric bill comes in.

It turns out that these graphic cards not only cost a fortune in and of themselves, they also require extreme amounts of electricity. This not only lowers the comparative advantage Venkat has over his peers, it also heats up his computer to dangerous levels.[14] To further complicate matters, now because of the increasing number of people worldwide mining for Bitcoin, Venkat's margins are getting slimmer and slimmer. Once upon a time, when very few people believed that Bitcoin could work, one could generate enough Bitcoin by solving problems by hand. Now, it's more difficult – and will get more complicated still!

As in everything in (capitalistic) life, if there is a demand, supply will follow, and that is exactly what happened with Bitcoin mining. Eventually, the process of mining became commercialized. Reprogrammed computer chips were developed and sold as alternatives to the (now) old gaming chips. Not only were these products much faster than their predecessors, they were exponentially faster than doing this work by hand. By today's standards these computer chips would be considered quite rudimentary solutions to mining for Bitcoin.

Eventually, a much faster option developed: application-specific integrated circuit chips, generally abbreviated to ASIC. These circuit chips are much faster than their predecessors and require less electricity per math problem, meaning that Venkat's electric bill would not cost more than the Bitcoin that he earned

---

[14] I've heard of cases of people even putting their computers in freezers because they were getting so heated from computer applications.

and that he won't have to put his laptop in a freezer to keep it from burning up. ASIC chips are another truly revolutionary development in the field of Bitcoin, but there is yet one more option that Venkat has that could allow him to make more money off Bitcoin mining.

TEAMING UP:

In the nascent years of Bitcoin, many miners were what we'd consider loners—they liked their computer world eschewing most other opportunities. But let's imagine that Venkat is a sociable fellow and has many friends who are interested in Bitcoin mining. How could they collectively generate more Bitcoin than their peers?

What has been developed over time is the process of '**pool mining.**' Pool miners are essentially a group of friends that get together to mine for Bitcoin. By gathering into groups to solve complex math equations, economies of scale become more important.

Whereas in the past, Venkat could simply buy an ASIC card and use that to mine for Bitcoin, by combining with friends, they can mine for Bitcoin at a quicker rate than everyone else, giving them a competitive edge. By conducting math problems in unison, they can mine for more Bitcoin at a faster rate than before. There's an interesting point here though.

As we can see, even if Venkat were a genius, he would never have been able to compete with the astronomical increase in technology, beginning with gaming chips and continuing with ASIC chips. No human can conduct enough math problems quickly enough to compete with computers, and later on, pools of computers. But how do computers solve these problems, and why does it consume so much electricity and labor? The answer may surprise you.

When Venkat solves a math problem, he does his best to get the answer correct on the first try. In order to do this, he uses previous mathematical skills to add or subtract a number. The ASIC chips, along with their predecessors do not work in such an efficient manner. Rather than solving a complex algorithm by using the same mathematical principles that Venkat uses, Bitcoin mining software solves problems through what computer scientists call *brute force*.

Brute force is essentially a method of problem solving where the computer randomly guesses answers to a math problem. Once the correct answer is guessed, the machine moves on to the next problem. As you can tell this is very unlike Venkat's method of problem solving, and as you likely guess, this is also how his electric bill becomes so high. Brute force, because of the high volume of guesses that ASIC chips conduct, becomes very energy intensive.

But why does Bitcoin have miners solving math problems?

This seems like an unusual way to circulate a currency. It is understood that fiat currency must be printed in order to circulate it; gold and silver logically have to be mined. But what happens when a computer is mining for Bitcoin? Essentially, **these math problems that Bitcoin miners solve are transactions going on within the blockchain network.**

Let's imagine that Miguel in Mexico City wants to give $50 to his friend, Barbara in Buenos Aires. Since it's impractical to convert from one currency to another, Miguel decides to give her money through Bitcoin. When this request gets placed through the blockchain network, computers mining for Bitcoin answer the calling through **brute force**. Once a computer solves the problem, it gets passed on to the next math equation, and so on.

So in essence what Bitcoin miners are doing is approving transactions along the blockchain. Because these transactions are done through computers and not manually—which are how many banks still operate—Bitcoin's transactions get solved 'immediately.' So Miguel's money reaches Barbara very quickly and much more efficiently than a single bank transaction would take.

MINING OFFERS YET ANOTHER LAYER OF SECURITY:

Mining in Bitcoin world offers a *proof of work*. Essentially, now the Bitcoin miners approved of Miguel's transfer to Barbara, he cannot double spend that money anywhere else.

In the same way he couldn't use those $50 at the grocery store and give them to Barbara, he cannot 'double dip' in the Bitcoin blockchain. If he were to try to do so, Miguel would have to out-compute all other miners in the network—a feat that is practically impossible.

This lends itself to a degree of security within the blockchain, as nobody can simply 'create' money out of nowhere. It also makes it more difficult to counterfeit the cryptocurrency. While counterfeiting dollars may be difficult enough because of the levels of security built into each unit, if there is such a way to counterfeit Bitcoin, it is unknown to me. There are simply too many eyes over the network. Also unlike fiat currency, an unknowing store clerk may inadvertently accept a fake bill without know it. This cannot be said for Bitcoin because every miner would know of any counterfeit charges or transactions.

MINERS = THE HUMAN CHECKS AND

BALANCES OF CRYPTOCURRENCY

Because of this, miners act as the Mint in fiat currency. They stamp their seals on each dollar and euro, ensuring the currency's authenticity. These Bitcoin miners are essentially notaries—but ensuring the validity of each transaction, they are keeping an eye over the entire blockchain.

Miners' jobs therefore, are very important, and as a reward for their labor, they are compensated in Bitcoin. This not only allows mining to be profitable; it also gives them an incentive to keep on mining. And here is the unique aspect of Bitcoin, the more miners there are on the blockchain, the more secure the network is, because miners keep an eye out over all Bitcoin transactions.

How Many Bitcoins Are There, and Will They Ever Stop Circulating Them?

Now that we have mentioned Bitcoin transactions, here's an important note regarding the number of Bitcoin in circulation: Remember how we mentioned that Bitcoin could be used to hedge against imprudent printing of fiat currency (the Zimbabwean dollar for example, with its 79 billion percent inflation rate)? Satoshi Nakamoto kept this in mind and limited the circulation to be 21 million Bitcoins. These Bitcoins would be released every ten minutes, which was initially how long it would take for the blockchain to reload.

Currently, it's much quicker due to the increase and popularity of mining. Originally however, there was a block reward for mining Bitcoin, which was a maximum of 50 per hour. Because of the ten-minute lag, a miner could only create six blocks per hour, which equates to 210,000 blocks in a year (assuming no breaks for the computer, of course). Additionally, every four years, the number of blocks created by mining will half.

For example, currently, the supply growth is held stagnant at 12.5 Bitcoins for every ten minutes. In four years, this number won't be at 12.5, but rather half of that—6.25 Bitcoins per ten minutes. Four years later, this number would also half: 3.125 Bitcoins per ten minutes, and so on, up until the magic number of 21 million Bitcoins is reached. It is predicted that the 21 million count will be reached between 2040 and 2050. For that math whiz reader out there who is interested in figuring out how all these numbers are related, here is the formula: 210,000 x 50 [(1 / (1 - 0.5)] = 21 million Bitcoin.

But what happens once 21 million Bitcoin is reached?

This is an interesting question. There are currently over 7 billion people in the world, and if Bitcoin's aim were to be a universal currency, then on average, every person would have 0.003 Bitcoins. Pretty pathetic, huh? Well, Satoshi has a secret. Once the magic number of 21 million is reached, the value of every Bitcoin will simultaneously be cut in half. Don't freak out though!
This does not mean that you will be left with half of the amount of money you had before. Far from it. The reason for the halving is to accommodate more and more users. The value of Bitcoin will eventually be determined not by the number of this cryptocurrency in circulation, but by the laws of supply and demand.
This means that it doesn't matter how many Bitcoin you actually have. What's important is how many you have in comparison to other users in the Bitcoin blockchain. This, in the end, is the true value of money. For better or worse, money is what some people have and others do not.

George Bernard Shaw's statement, quoted in the introduction, is still true: *lack of* money is the root of all evil. Now that we have a rudimentary understanding of how Bitcoin works, let's look at the more interesting aspect of this cryptocurrency— how to invest in it.

How Do I Invest In Bitcoin?

If the previous section on Bitcoin mining left you a bit confused, don't worry at all. There is another, more efficient manner of making money off Bitcoin: investing.

Now clearly this comes with some caveats. There is the possibility that when investing in any endeavor, the individual may lose all or some of their money, and Bitcoin is no different. There is something to be said for not putting all of your eggs in one basket, and Bitcoin has the potential to be an exploding basket.

For professional advice on investing in Bitcoin, it is suggested that you speak to your financial advisor. On a less professional note, here is some information on how Bitcoin has risen from being worth nothing to rising over $10,000 per Bitcoin at the end of 2017!

Figure 4: Value of Bitcoin (Source: Bitcoin.com)[15]

---

[15] Information taken from https://charts.bitcoin.com/chart/price

Check out the value of Bitcoin over the past year. Keep in mind that this chart only shows 2017. *Figure 4* only shows the trajectory of Bitcoin in 2017, but you get the idea. It was worth practically nothing in 2012 and now ranges in the $10,000 area.

Before we get too ahead of ourselves, let's remember that there are two dependent variables working against each other in this chart. First, obviously is the value of Bitcoin against the dollar. Second, and perhaps more hidden, is the changing value of the dollar.

However, unlike Bitcoin's meteoric rise, the dollar has been slightly increasing in value against other currencies over the past few years. Clearly, it's Bitcoin's value that has greatly increased and not insane dollar inflation. At the risk of getting rid of this rosy picture, let's look at another graph illustrating the rise of Bitcoin from 2011 to this September.

Figure 5: Rise of Bitcoin 2011-2017 (Source: CoinDesk 2017)[16]

---

[16] This graph was taken from https://www.coindesk.com/price/

In this graph, we generally see the rise of Bitcoin, especially in 2017. However, let's take a look at what happened in 2014. We observe a strong increase in value from being worth absolutely nothing to $1000 in a matter of a few months. Then, almost immediately, we see the price drop precipitously.

This is known as a financial or economic bubble, similar to the ones that we saw in the housing market before the 2008 and the dot-com boom in the 1990s. A **bubble** occurs when the trading of a specific asset strongly exceeds the real value of those assets.

For example, during the recent housing crisis that affected most of the United States, homes were selling for double or triple of what their actual prices were. So if a home that originally cost $200,000 was sold in 2007, someone would have likely bought it for half a million dollars. But, no matter, people simply kept on buying! And if that happens, property owners are simply going to charge even higher prices.

Eventually some investors realized that the housing market could no longer support such ballooning price tags for single-family dwellings, and the values of homes came crashing down (and the stock market with it). The values of these homes perhaps dropped to less than what it cost to build them. So what happened to the family that bought a home for half a million dollars? They are paying off a home at a mortgage for a home worth $500,000 when, in reality, their home is only worth $200,000.

When situations like these occur, the 'bubble' bursts. Here's the tricky part: we never really know *beforehand* when the bubble will burst, or if there's a bubble at all. We can only tell after the fact.

So when we see the Bitcoin market only from 2013 to 2014, we see a huge rise in value, just to watch it drop again (there's the bubble bursting). However, if we see Bitcoin's trajectory from 2014 to the present day, we can spot another meteoric rise in value.

Is this a bubble? The answer to that question is way out of the scope of this book. Keep in mind that for physical products (such as a home), there is definitely some inherent value to it. But what about Bitcoin? There is nothing physical that an investor can palpably touch? No, the value of Bitcoin lies in whatever everyone says its worth.

Don't be too afraid though. The same holds true for the $100 bill that only cost 12 cents to make. No rational person would ever trade a $100 bill for twelve cents, even though that's its production value. Rather, the $100 bill is worth exactly that because we all collectively agree that you can buy $100 worth of stuff in exchange for it. The same is true for gold, silver, gems, and yes, Bitcoin.

So if public opinion is what largely drives the value of Bitcoin, what influences public opinion? Specifically, what if Bitcoin begins receiving a whole lot of bad press? What would happen to the value of Bitcoin then?

Interestingly and paradoxically enough, the better a stock is performing, the *more* criticism and negative press it receives! The same rules seem to apply to Bitcoin.

Take a look at what Kerry Close stated publicly in *Time* magazine right after the Bitcoin bubble of 2014: "virtual currency is known for wild fluctuations in price. The value of one Bitcoin—which was created in 2008 by an anonymous programmer or group of programmers—reached its all-time high of $1,165.89 in November 2013 before taking a major dive" (Close 2017).[17] Bad press, no? While Close clearly believed that the value of Bitcoin was going to nosedive, he, along with many other financial investors and analysts, were dead wrong.

Where they were correct is in recognizing Bitcoin's notorious volatility. In the same article, Kerry Close astutely notes that prices "have more or less inched up, and at the turn of the year, they started to approach record highs. On Thursday, the value of a bitcoin reached $1,153.02. However, later Thursday morning, prices suddenly fell by about $200."

This sort of volatility, while it does not show up in the graphs above, does occur on a daily basis. For someone to successfully invest in Bitcoin, they must be prepared to receive extraordinary gains, but also know that they may lose a lot of that money overnight.

There is no shortage of this type of bad press for Bitcoin, but does that mean that you should not invest in it? That's something only you can answer based on the amount of risk you're willing to handle in your life– we are simply here to inform you of trends. It is strongly suggested that you seek financial advise before making large investments of any kind.

There is one final and important note in investing in Bitcoin. This cryptocurrency is not the single monolith that many expect. Right after Kerry Close's negative comments on Bitcoin, there was a hidden development in the cryptocurrency world. Perhaps coincidentally, Bitcoin went through what's called a *hard fork* and developed a new cryptocurrency called Bitcoin Cash.

---

[17] Information taken from http://time.com/money/4623650/bitcoin-invest/

What is Bitcoin Cash?

Just when we thought that Bitcoins would only exist in cyberspace, there comes an oxymoron called **Bitcoin Cash**. Before we delve into what this is, let's first examine the term *hard fork* that led us to this. Remember that when cryptocurrency enthusiasts talk about Bitcoin, they like to throw some of these terms at you. Generally, they are simple terms and *hard fork* is no different.

A **hard fork** *occurs when there is a radical change in the operating protocol of a cryptocurrency rendering a set of transactions valid*. What this means is that Bitcoin is essentially dividing in two and creating another blockchain that would make many transactions valid that otherwise were not so.

This permanent fork in the blockchain suddenly allows streams of income to enter from another group or location. A good way to think of it is like a valve. When you open your sink, you allow water to flow from the pipes and through your faucet. Once you close it, no water is flowing.

The same concept holds true for Bitcoin's blockchain, and because of this, if you think you can suddenly double your money, you're dead wrong. In Bitcoin's hard fork it created another currency called **Bitcoin Cash**.

Bitcoin Cash works exactly like Bitcoin, with its own distributed ledger and miners circulating currency while keeping an eye out for malicious transactions. Also similar to Bitcoin is that it is a P2P compatible currency with no centralized control. So how does it differ from its parent cryptocurrency?

Bitcoin Cash has the potential to be 'scaled.' But what does 'scaling' mean in the cryptocurrency world? Luckily, its definition is the same in business.

Let's work with an example. Imagine that your aunt, Jennifer, is looking to bake some cookies. It takes her an hour to mix the dough, preheat the oven, and bake one cookie. While Jennifer may be full after she eats her one cookie, this isn't the most efficient use of her time and resources.

Soon your aunt decides to buy a larger cookie tray and get the ingredients in bulk. Jennifer soon realizes that while it took her an hour to make one cookie, it takes only slightly more time (say, an hour and five minutes) to bake a dozen cookies. Now she has enough for herself and her family.

But what if Aunt Jennifer wants to make a business out of this? She could invest in a larger oven that can bake a hundred cookies at a time, get better deals is she buys in bulk from providers, and make one hundred cookies per hour. Now she has enough for herself, her family, and to sell. Notice what Jennifer did here. She realized that it took more or less the same amount of time to bake one cookie as it did to bake one hundred cookies.

This is what we mean by scalable. In the cryptocurrency world however, we're not talking one hundred cookies. It must be just as easy to conduct ten transactions, as it is to conduct ten million transactions. This is what Bitcoin Cash brings to the table.

What Is the Difference Between Bitcoin and Bitcoin Cash:

The main difference between Bitcoin Cash and its predecessor is that Bitcoin Cash raises its block size from one megabyte to eight megabytes. This allows for speedier transactions to be conducted along the blockchain. Furthermore, "Bitcoin Cash introduces a new way of signing transactions. This also brings additional benefits such as input value signing for improved hardware wallet security, and elimination of the quadratic hashing problem" (Bitcoin Cash 2017).[18]

Borrowing from the same article, Bitcoin Cash also has wipeout/replay protection. In the case that "two chains persist, Bitcoin Cash minimizes user disruption, and permits safe and peaceful coexistence of the two chains, with well thought out replay and wipeout protection." This hard fork was implemented for many reasons. Some of these reasons, detailed below, will give us further insight into the world of this cryptocurrency.

BLOCKCHAIN SCALABILITY:

We have to remember that even though 2008 was not so long ago, it is a lifetime in the cryptocurrency world. When Satoshi first developed Bitcoin, the most advanced processing system at the time allowed for a one-megabyte limit of data per block, which equates to three transactions per second. With the eight-megabyte limit, transactions can be conducted much faster. But so what?

Why did Bitcoin's stock simply skyrocket with the advent of Bitcoin Cash? This doesn't happen when Apple, Microsoft, or Dell create a faster computer. Their stocks stay the same (or perhaps slightly increase over time) with the development of each new technological advance.

Why is Bitcoin so different simply because it can now process transactions at a faster rate? It's important to note that this is the first time Bitcoin has changed its blockchain. While there were many questions as to how this would occur, the fact that Bitcoin simply developed Bitcoin Cash and 'forked' seemed to show investors that it was quite capable and willing to change

---

[18] Information taken from https://www.bitcoincash.org

according to advances in technology; they already knew this about Apple, Microsoft, and Dell.

Second, they noticed that mining has been increasing at a faster and faster pace, yet Bitcoin remained the same. With Bitcoin Cash, investors saw that this cryptocurrency could be enhanced and adapted to advances in Bitcoin mining.

NEW IMPROVEMENTS FOR INCREASED SECURITY:

According to Bitcoin Cash's website, they have singled out new features that are worth noting, including chain scalability (the ability to process many more transactions at once), new transaction signatures, new difficulty adjustment algorithms, and decentralized development.

For new transaction signatures, they adopted a new *SigHash* to provide replay protection, improve wallet security, and eliminate a former quadratic hashing problem. Furthermore, regarding the new difficulty adjustment algorithm, they state that this is a "responsive proof-of-work difficulty adjustment that allows miners to migrate from the legacy Bitcoin chain as desired [To Bitcoin Cash], while providing protection against hashrate fluctuations" (Bitcoin Cash 2017).[19]

DECENTRALIZED DEVELOPMENT:

Finally, they had to deal with the problem of decentralized development. Bitcoin Cash notes that with "multiple independent teams of developers providing software implementations, the

---

[19] All of the information from this paragraph is taken from https://www.bitcoincash.org/#about

future is secure. Bitcoin Cash is resistant to political and social attacks on protocol development. No single group or project can control it. The bitcoin-ml (mailing list) is a good venue for making proposals for changes that require coordination across development teams" (ibid.).

WORLD MARKET VALUE OF BITCOIN:

This last point is important, especially for international investors. Unlike the euro, peso, or rupee or others that may be influenced by external forces occurring within the country, Bitcoin Cash is driven by the world market value of its currency. We saw the value of Bitcoin compared to the dollar in the graphs above, but if we were to compare it to the value of the Venezuelan bolivar, we'd be seeing much higher profits for Bitcoin.

This is not because Bitcoin's value has increased. Rather because of strong inflationary practices of the Venezuelan government, their local currency has decreased in value. But if Bitcoin remains the same, or increases in value, what should Venezuelans do? The ones with access to Internet would do well to save their money in Bitcoin rather than in their local currency, which is going to be worth less every single day.

This is all interesting, but how do I get my hands on Bitcoin?

Similar to physical currencies, there is a specific way for someone to save Bitcoin for future transactions. If there is one thing about the world that Bitcoin users know (or should know), it's that one should never over-inundate people with complex information. The world can only allow one change at a time.

BITCOIN WALLETS:

Cryptocurrencies were revolutionary enough, so in order to make people more comfortable with them, they developed **'wallets'** for Bitcoin. These wallets serve the same function and operate in the same way that regular wallets do – they keep your money. There is also an element of anonymity in Bitcoin wallets that we do not have with credit cards and checks. Bitcoin encrypts the user's information, rendering it much more difficult to hack a single user. Below is a simple diagram showing how Bitcoin encrypts personal information so that hackers are left with a tougher time in attempting to steal someone's information.

Figure 6: Example of how Bitcoin Encrypts Information (Source: Bitcoin Core 2017)[20]

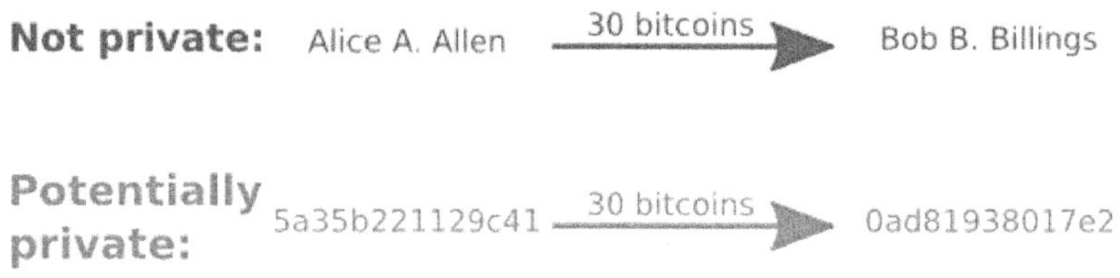

Not private: Alice A. Allen —— 30 bitcoins ——▶ Bob B. Billings

Potentially private: 5a35b221129c41 —— 30 bitcoins ——▶ 0ad81938017e2

USING BITCOIN WALLETS:

Now that we are a bit more comfortable with the potential security benefits of using Bitcoin, let's see how different Bitcoin wallets can be used to buy and sell products online. For the sake of simplicity, we are going to examine each wallet from simplest to most advanced. The average Bitcoin user would be happy with the

---

[20] Chart taken from https://bitcoin.org/en/bitcoin-core/features/privacy

basic wallets, but in case you're interested in running a business with Bitcoin, we are including some of the more advanced wallet options as well.

There are multiple Bitcoin wallets that you can keep your money in. Without going too in depth into these wallets, let's take a brief look at how they are similar and different from one another. To take a look at these wallets, first visit *https://bitcoin.org/en/getting-started* and pick the *"Choose Your Wallet"* icon. Instead of going in the order shown in their website, we are going to analyze these wallets from simplest to most complex.

BITCOIN CORE:

First up is Bitcoin Core. This is the easiest and simplest wallet to understand. It offers the high level of security that we have come to associate with distributed ledgers, but none of the bells and whistles that we would see in other wallets. One of the downsides of this wallet is that it occupies a lot of space in your hard drive.

Additionally, according to their website, the security risks exists because "this wallet can be loaded on computers which are vulnerable to malware. Securing your computer, using a strong passphrase, moving most of your funds to cold storage, or enabling two-factor authentication can make it harder to steal your bitcoins" (Bitcoin Core 2017).[21] However, don't be discouraged! All Bitcoin wallets receive the same information on that level.

---

[21] Quote taken from https://bitcoin.org/en/wallets/desktop/windows/bitcoincore/

BITCOIN KNOTS:

The next wallet that we will analyze is **Bitcoin Knots**, which is considered similar to Bitcoin Core. The main difference between Bitcoin Core and Bitcoin Knots is that the latter can hold multiple accounts in the same wallet.

Let's imagine that John and Mary are married to each other. If they decide to keep their cryptocurrency finances in one place, they can use this wallet. However, should they want to use it for different reasons or decide to split their accounts, they can still log into one account and see different numbers per account, while still using the same wallet.

With Bitcoin Core, this would be impossible as its one wallet per person. As for downsides with Bitcoin Knots, it's the same as with every computer: if your laptop is compromised, there is a great chance that your security information would also be in jeopardy. Both Bitcoin Core and Bitcoin Knots are useful tools for the casual person looking to buy and sell products with Bitcoin. Here are some more advanced wallets that can help you take your business to the next level.

GREEN ADDRESS:

GreenAddress loves to boast its user-friendliness as Bitcoin wallet. Different from *Electrum*, which uses a decentralized server, **GreenAddress** has the classic centralized system. According to the Bitcoin website on GreenAddress, this "wallet is loaded from a remote location.

This means that whenever you use your wallet, you need to trust the developers not to steal or lose your bitcoins in an incident on their site. Using a browser extension or mobile app, if available, can reduce that risk" (Bitcoin 2017).[22]

Because of this centralized security system along with the third party that you Bitcoin involves, GreenAddress is better for personal use rather than business use. I highly suggest that this wallet not be used for any official business transactions, but it should be fine with financial transactions between family and friends.

BITHER:

Bither is a relatively simple wallet that could be used by individuals, professionals, or companies. It operates well under iOS, Windows, Android, Mac, and Linux platforms and has a 'cold storage' option. Many Bitcoin wallets tout this feature, so it's worth examining. When someone is operating in 'hot mode,' they are essentially online.

This means that any typical cell phone, once the Bither wallet is downloaded, will be considered *'hot.'* On the other hand, *'cold mode'* is when a computer is offline. Some Bitcoin wallets can allow you to backup information on a 'cold' device—meaning that essentially you have information stored on a computer that is not connected to the Internet. This allows for an extra layer of security for your Bitcoins.

ELECTRUM:

Another relatively simple wallet is **Electrum**, which is

---

[22] Quote taken from https://bitcoin.org/en/wallets/desktop/windows/greenaddress/

famous for its speed and rapidity. Somewhat similar to the blockchain that Bitcoin uses, Electrum's servers are decentralized, which means that there's no lag in the system.
It also offers the hot and cold options that we saw with Bither.

Furthermore, there is an interesting advancement to Electrum that many of the next wallets espouse: **they have two-factor authentication**. Again, this is another cryptocurrency term designed to either confuse you, or leave you with a sense of security.

Here's an easy example: Noelle is accepting Bitcoins from her friends and uses Electrum as her wallet. Just like with any computer login, she needs to present a username and a password. With most websites, this is enough to allow you to enter into their system. However, with two-factor authentication, they would either send Noelle an email, text, or phone call to make sure that she's indeed the person who is attempting to log into her account. This is that 'two-factor' part of the authentication. Most of the next wallets have this system built into their programs.

ARMORY:

Armory is another Bitcoin wallet with many of the features we have seen above. Similar to Bither, Armory allows hot and cold storage to increase safety. For their cold storage option, you "can create your wallet on a computer that never touches the Internet, yet still manage the wallet from an online computer with minimal risk of an attacker stealing your funds" (Armory 2017).[23]

This wallet is clearly meant for businesses, as it would only be a fruitful investment to pay for an offline computer if you know that you're going to be conducting many high-end transactions for

---

[23] Information taken from https://www.bitcoinarmory.com/cold-storage/

your business. On the other hand, if you're simply looking to buy stuff and exchange money in a P2P fashion between friends and family, this wallet seems a bit too advanced for such simple transactions.

ArcBit:

The next wallet that we are going to examine is **ArcBit**. This wallet is also featured in the Bitcoin website and has the traditional cold wallet mechanism that we are finding in many storage options.

The main difference between ArcBit and other wallets is that is espouses a remote wallet option. Think of it this way: your wallet is working for you despite the fact that you are not physically next to it. Clearly, this can only work in cyberspace, but that's why it's so effective.

Your wallet is essentially "loaded from a remote location. This means that whenever you use your wallet, you need to trust the developers not to steal or lose your bitcoins in an incident on their site. Using a browser extension or mobile app, if available, can reduce that risk" (Bitcoin 2017).[24]

Similar to other Bitcoin wallets, ArcBit "gives you full control over your Bitcoins. This means no third party can freeze or lose your funds. You are however still responsible for securing and backing up your wallet" (ibid.). According to the Bitcoin website, there is another positive aspect with choosing ArcBit as a wallet.

They state that ArcBit "provides fee suggestions which are based on current network conditions which you can override. This means that this wallet will help you choose the appropriate fee so

---

[24] Information taken from https://bitcoin.org/en/wallets/desktop/windows/arcbit/

that your transactions are confirmed in a timely manner without paying more than you have to, but ultimately gives you control if you want to override the suggestion" (ibid.).

BitGo:

The next wallet that we are to evaluate is **BitGo**. This wallet, similar to Armory, is designed for business use, meaning that there are higher levels of security, but at the cost of expediency. It is a multi-sig wallet, meaning that multiple signatures are required to enter into it. Furthermore, it offers the two-factor authorization feature that we have seen in previous wallets.

This wallet also has developed an even more advanced version of itself, *BitGo Instant*. Again, this wallet is best-equipped for large-scale business use, rather than individual or private usage, as its features may be too advanced for the casual transactions between family and friends.

Their website (which seems much more developed than other Bitcoin wallet websites, proudly states that BitGo "allows on-chain, zero confirm, instant transactions between participants. Before BitGo Instant, typical transactions took 10 minutes or more to be recorded in a block by miners" (BitGo 2017).[25]

This transaction must then be approved by the miners in Bitcoin, and previously understood as *zero-confirm*. If it weren't for the security features on this wallet, transactions such as these would be treading into dangerous waters because "without BitGo

---

[25] Information taken from https://www.bitgo.com/solutions#wallet

Instant's guarantee, it is possible for the sender to spend the money elsewhere before the transaction is confirmed" (ibid.).

These multiple confirmations would be problematic for the casual user, but not for companies. Furthermore, this solves the potential and proverbial problem of double dipping. The wallet does not allow for someone to spend a Bitcoin on one product and *simultaneously* spend that *same* Bitcoin on another product.
mSIGNA

Finally, the last wallet that we must analyze is **mSIGNA**, another ridiculously complex name for a Bitcoin wallet. Similar to BitGo, their website seems much more advanced than the basic Bitcoin wallets. According to them, mSIGNA is "a next-generation multi-signature wallet. It supports the best security practices in the industry and is rated amongst the most secure wallets by bitcoin.org.

While an advanced tool, it is easy to use. It is very fast, and its inherent scalability offers enterprise-level solutions. And best of all, it's a free and open source" (mSINGA 2017).[26] Other wallets may soon be offering this option, but mSIGNA is the only one that I know of that also offers Litecoin capabilities.

Perhaps there are wallets that are also compatible with Ethereum, Dogecoin, and Ripple, but they do not advertise it much. We will examine the possibilities of other cryptocurrencies in the next question. As for mSIGNA, it also seems much more advanced in its usability and user-friendly account. Below is a snapshot illustrating the difference mSIGNA and Bitcoin Knots.

Figure 7: Differences between mSIGNA and Bitcoin Knots

---

[26] Quote taken from https://ciphrex.com

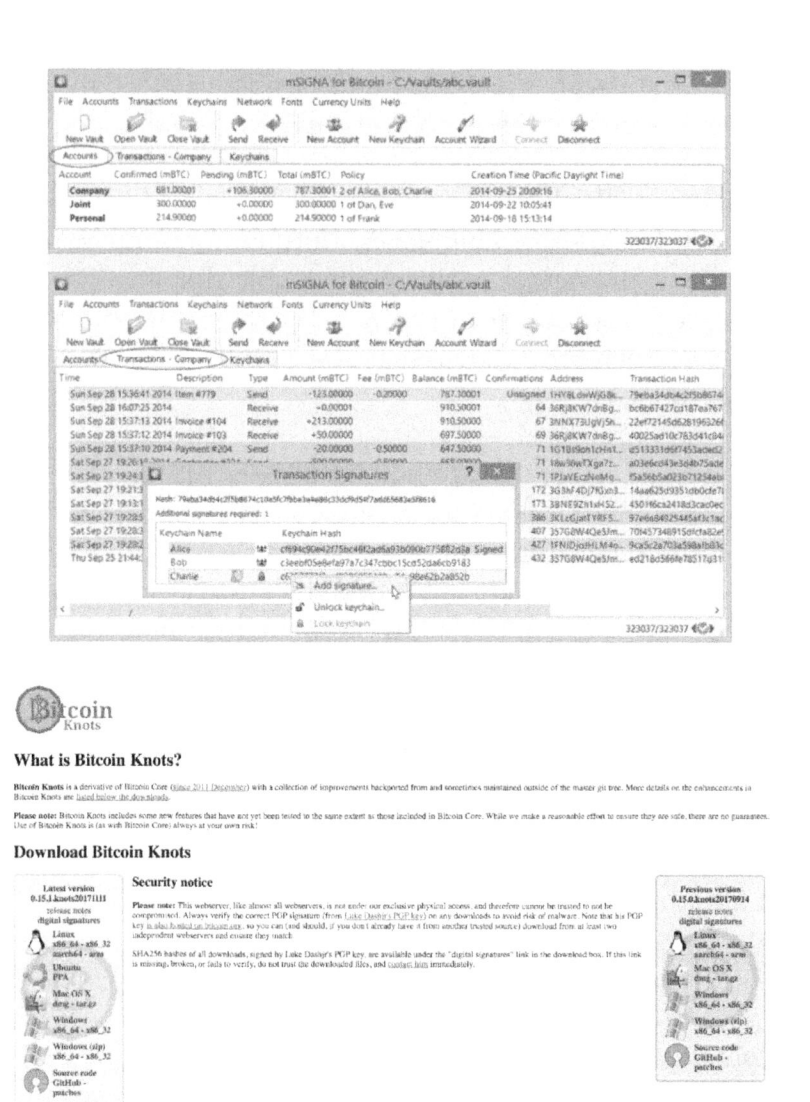

As we can see, while mSIGNA offers an accountant-style wallet with accounts in-and-out, while Bitcoin Knots hasn't seemed to update its profile in a while. That said; don't judge a book by its cover. The most important thing for you to do when choosing a wallet is to make sure that it serves your purposes, despite the graphics.

For complete details on the differences between wallets, I strongly encourage you to visit the Bitcoin wallet website, found at https://bitcoin.org/en/choose-your-wallet. Much of the information here is taken from their website. They also break down the differences in wallets into different tables that allow you to evaluate the pros and cons of each wallet to best pick which option best suits your needs. The next question that we are going to answer is an interesting one, and if you're interested in investing in other cryptocurrencies other than Bitcoin, it is for you.

Are there any other cryptocurrencies other than Bitcoin?

As we have noted time and again, Bitcoin has gained quite a success over the past few years. And, as always in history, whenever there is a stellar success with one industry, many others come in seeking to take advantage of their unprecedented gains. Bitcoin and cryptocurrencies are no different. If you're interested in learning about and investing in cryptocurrencies, then this section is for you. First, while Bitcoin takes the lion's share of crypto-enthusiasm, there is another currency that gives Bitcoin a good run for its money—Ethereum.

ETHEREUM:

Vitalik Buterin, Ethereum's founder, took advantage of the increase in technology from when Bitcoin was first created in 2008 to when Ethereum entered the market in 2013. Because of this, Ethereum espouses a much more advanced blockchain algorithm than its predecessor. And while it competes with Bitcoin as a cryptocurrency, its true claim to fame is elsewhere. Before we analyze the deep differences between Bitcoin and Ethereum, let's see how they both relate as cryptocurrencies.

Just like any cryptocurrency, Ethereum is founded and based upon the blockchain network. In fact, it would be hard to imagine a cryptocurrency that didn't run using blockchain technology. Unlike Bitcoin, whose currency is simply based on supply and demand, with miners creating more and more Bitcoin as we speak, users implementing Ethereum create their own currency, called *ethers*.

These **ethers** are simply units of currency to be employed along the Ethereum blockchain. Bitcoin may be attempting to compete with every government-issue currency (pounds, euros, dollars, yen, yuan, etc.), but Ethereum is sidelining these problems.

According to Coindesk, ethers were not designed to be converted from one currency to another. Rather, they are "meant to pay for specific actions on the Ethereum network, with users receiving it for using their computing power to validate transactions and for contributing to its development" (Coindesk 2017).[27]

Due to it's advanced technology Ethereum is ahead of Bitcoin in its response time. Remember how Bitcoin took 10 minutes to reload? **Ethereum can do the same transaction in 17 seconds!** This means that transactions are essentially 'live' when you're working on them. But how can we apply this to regular life, and how different is it really from Bitcoin?

So How is Ethereum (ETH) really Different from

---

[27] Quote obtained from https://www.coindesk.com/what-to-know-trading-ethereum/

Bitcoin?

SMART CONTRACTS:

Ethereum allows the user to create what's called **'smart contracts'** with their platform. A **smart contract** essentially works in the same way a regular contract work, but allows itself to be edited over time. Unlike a paper contract, that would have to be printed out and distributed with every iteration of the contract, a smart contract works a lot like a GoogleDocs document that anyone can edit with changes before they're agreed upon.

 Let's imagine a simple scenario: Kathi in New Zealand wants to sell her condo to Terence, living in South Africa. They could physically meet up and agree upon a contract, or pass emails back and forth up until a deal is reached.

 However, in order to do this, they would have to go through dozens of middlemen, ranging from realtors, attorneys, insurance companies, and so on. With Ethereum, Kathi just has to create a smart contract that both she and Terence can manipulate. Once they agree upon terms, they can amend the contract as required. Then it's time to sign.

 Because smart contracts generate an encrypted code that is unique to any contract, both Kathi and Terence know that they are signing the exact same document. **If even a comma is different, the Ethereum smart contract would generate a completely different encrypted code**, so both parties would be aware that they're signing different contracts. This would be impossible with regular paper and ink. Plus the parties would have to pay for extra individuals to be in the agreement, as lawyers, accountants, and staff would be necessary.

 While the example of buying a condo is given here, there could be an almost infinite number of ways that smart contracts, using Ethereum, can revolutionize the way they conduct business.

Smart contracts can be used for leases, rental agreements, deeds for next of kin, and so on.

The other way that Ethereum has become revolutionary is that it automates every single aspect of smart contracts. Instead of having humans review documents and line items, computers do the work for them. This allows mortgage companies, financial institutions, and investment firms to save a lot of money on back-end employees that would severely affect their bottom line. This automation also eliminates the possibility of human error, and since the network oversees itself, then security is much tighter than with a centralized database.

Outside of Bitcoin, Ethereum is by far the next cryptocurrency taking a big leap in the stock market. Below is the chart from 2017, where we see Ethereum jump from a few cents to $400 in 2017.

Figure 8: Ethereum Price (2017)

This information, taken from Coindesk, shows how Ethereum has increased in value over the past year. Let's analyze this a bit.

First, as we can see, while the value of Ethereum has really kicked off, there is no comparison between Ethereum's value and

Bitcoin's meteoric rise. However, while there are differences in terms of magnitude, their direction is the same—up.

Let's look a bit deeper into the graphs: Sometime in July, Ethereum's value clearly increased at a quick pace. Then from August to September, we saw its value decrease substantially.[28] Take a look at Bitcoin's chart and you will see something similar. Then, with the advent of Bitcoin Cash and Bitcoin's value continuing to skyrocket, Ethereum seems to be riding Bitcoin's coattails.

Investors should always keep in mind that there are many variables influencing the prices of any commodity, but since all cryptocurrencies fall under one specific part of the stock market, they are influenced by many of the same issues.

As you will recall, the main issue that will not influence cryptocurrencies are crises 'on the ground' that would influence fiat currency. If you're interested in investing, I suggest you take a look at Kraken, Coinbase, or Bittrex for platforms on where to invest your cryptocurrencies.

We are now going to move on to another cryptocurrency—Ripple. However, before we continue, you should know that **there are over 900 cryptocurrencies**, most of which are not worth a penny in the stock market. This means that if you invest small amounts in many of these, you may be able to see some gains. Now let's move on to Ripple.

RIPPLE:

Ripple is an interesting cryptocurrency, and solves an interesting issue. Remember how we were mentioning that it

---

[28] For what it's worth, the biggest problem I have with any of the cryptocurrencies right now is people are treating them like they're stocks. They're not stocks. I think that once the amateur traders realize they aren't trading stocks, they'll get out of the market and the bubble will burst.

currently takes a bank three to five business days to conduct a simple transaction between friends? This is the issue that Ripple is trying to solve.

Here's the process between banks every time you want to send money over to friends. When you extract money, the bank has to process it, meaning that they must subtract that exact amount from your bank account. This money is then transferred to your friend's bank account; always making sure that it's the exact amount.
Meanwhile, these figures need to be checked by a computer and by employees to ensure that they are identical. Multiply this process out thousands of times and it's really a miracle that they manage to do all of this in three to five business days. But where does Ripple come into play?

As was previously stated, Ripple was created by banks for banks. This means that it was developed as a proxy currency so that trades can occur between financial institutions in seconds and not days.

Let's briefly refer back to the introduction: remember those Chinese merchants who were growing tired of lugging around heavy copper coins around the South China Sea? What they developed was paper money, designed to replace the copper coins while at sea, and then traded for currency when back on land. This allowed the Chinese merchants to carry more cargo and not worry about their currency sinking to the bottom of the ocean if anything happened (they actually had to worry about it flying away from them in a strong wind).
Because they used paper, even if only for sailing at sea, they were able to gain a competitive advantage over other merchants. Ripple is essentially offering the 21st century version of this for banks. They have a proxy currency for P2P transactions between friends, families, and institutions. This is another form of what is called **FinTech**.

FinTech:

FinTech, or financial technology, is another term loved by cryptocurrency users. Financial technology can mean almost anything, but its most important quality is that it makes conducting transactions between individuals, institutions, and banks easier and more efficient.

The Chinese merchants collectively deciding to use paper instead of copper coins is a rudimentary example of FinTech.

Ripple offers this sort of service, and its goal "is to enable people to break free from the 'walled gardens' of financial networks – i.e., credit cards, banks, PayPal and other institutions that restrict access with fees, charges for currency exchanges and processing delays" (Coindesk 2013).[29] Tearing down these 'walled gardens' is another form of advancing speeds and performance of currencies, which is what FinTech is all about.

The other main difference between Ripple, Ethereum, and Bitcoin is how these currencies are produced: While Bitcoin involves mining and you can create your own currency with Ethereum (ethers), Ripple takes a very small sum of money per transaction and puts it into the network. This is how it is reproduced, and it's quite an insignificant sum.

Furthermore, the "amount is destroyed rather than retained. The deduction is meant as to safeguard against the system being swamped by any one individual who might try to put through millions of transactions at once" (Coindesk 2013). Additionally, because all of the Ripple in the world already exists (it is a pre-mined cryptocurrency, as if this couldn't get any weirder), there is no way to create currency.

---

[29] Information taken from **https://www.coindesk.com/10-things-you-need-to-know-about-ripple/**

Instead, they burn off a bit from each transaction, which works in exactly the opposite way than every other currency! You're still creating demand, but instead of starting with zero and increasing supply, you're now starting off with 100 billion Ripples, and lowering the number from there onward. With Ripple, you're burning cash and making money at the same time!

LITECOIN:

Let's now look at what seems to be Bitcoin 2.0—Litecoin. Admittedly, there is little to get excited about regarding Litecoin as it's so similar to its predecessor, who is, by the way, much more famous and valuable. However, there are plenty of similarities between these two coins that it's worth mentioning Litecoin as a potential supplement to Bitcoin. Let's see how the differences play out:

First of all, you can get your Litecoin at https://litecoin.org. Similar to Bitcoin, it's primarily a P2P interface adopting blockchain technology and working as a cryptocurrency. If you go to their website, you'll find that Litecoin "enables instant, near-zero cost payments to anyone in the world. Litecoin is an open source, global payment network that is fully decentralized without any central authorities. Mathematics secures the network and empowers individuals to control their own finances. Litecoin features faster transaction confirmation times and improved storage efficiency than the leading math-based currency" (Litecoin 2017).[30] The decentralized aspect of Litecoin, along with the 'math-based currency' that they are touting is quite similar to Bitcoin.

---

[30] Quote taken from https://litecoin.org

What's the Difference Between Bitcoin and Litecoin?

One of the main differences between Bitcoin and Litecoin is that while Bitcoin uses SHA-256 (along with most other cryptocurrencies) as its coding language, Litecoin implements another language, called *Scrypt*. While for investors, there is hardly a difference (or importance) in the coding language that these cryptocurrencies use there are some back-end differences worth noting that may influence investment.

It is generally agreed upon that Scrypt is an extremely safe computer coding language. While its safety may be more pronounced than SHA-256, there is little evidence that SHA-256 has ever been unsafe. Here's the other part of the story: SHA-256 has been tested out 'in the world' so to speak, and because of this, we have more evidence that it is a successful program for computer coding.

Scrypt, on the other hand, due to its relative newness, remains an unknown quantity. It's arguably safer than SHA-256, but hasn't had the public testing that SHA-256 has gone through.

The second difference between Bitcoin and Litecoin is the number of Litecoins in existence. As opposed to Ripple, which is already pre-mined, and Ethereum's 'create your own currency' policy, Litecoin and Bitcoin's coins must be mined.

You will recall that Bitcoin had 21 million coins as its cap. No more Bitcoins were ever to be mined, but if demand continued to increase, there would be a halving of each Bitcoin (not its value, just number). This could continue *ad infinitum*. Litecoin has announced that there will be 84 million Litecoin in existence; exactly four times as many Bitcoin.

But why is this the case? Well, Litecoin was developed a few years after Bitcoin, using pretty much the same formula but with better technology. Because of this, the time it takes to create a Litecoin is exactly four times as fast as with Bitcoin. Whereas the average Bitcoin miner had to wait the usual ten minutes for the block to be completed, with Litecoin, this can be done in two and a half minutes.

However, there is no comparison between Litecoin and Ethereum's seventeen-second lag. Because of this faster Litecoin reproduction, developers can engage in even quicker transaction times. Miners in Litecoin's world are rewarded with twenty-five Litecoins for every block in the blockchain network.

Similar to Bitcoin, the extant Litecoins gets halved every 4 years (sound familiar? Just like Bitcoin). This means that for every 840,000 blocks, the Litecoins get halved. Predictably, Litecoin uses the same formula as Bitcoin, leaving us with 84 million Litecoin.

There clearly are some differences between Bitcoin and Litecoin, but because they are so similar, the gain of one may be the demise of the other. This would not be the case with Ethereum and Ripple, which are completely different and seek to solve completely separate problems, smart contracts and bank-to-bank transfers, respectively.

While there is no denying that Litecoin is a faster, more reliable, currency than Bitcoin, is it perhaps too similar to its predecessor? Investors should feel comfortable in investing in Litecoin after witnessing the success of Bitcoin, but the million-dollar question is whether or not there will be a market for Litecoin given Bitcoin's unprecedented success.

Will Bitcoin completely replace fiat currency (regular money)?

This is a speculative question to be sure, but let's give it a shot. First things first—only time will tell if Bitcoin (or any other cryptocurrency) will replace fiat currency (regular money). We will first examine arguments for why it may well replace physical cash, and then we will examine arguments for why it will not.

ARGUMENTS FOR THE REPLACEMENT OF FIAT CURRENCY WITH CRYPTOCURRENCY:

Money is simply a tool by which we buy and sell our products. As we have seen throughout the course of this book, money itself has little or no value. What matters is what money represents. As proof of this, it costs the United States Mint 12 cents to make a $100 bill. Clearly the production cost of the bill was only 12 cents, but its value is so much more. However, we are encountering some very real problems with physical currency.

For example, it costs more money to make a penny than the penny is worth. This may still be a bit of a joke, but what happens when this is the case for the nickel, dime, quarter, and dollar? Bitcoin has the potential to replace physical currency *production values*.

What does this mean? Because Bitcoin mining uses up no natural resources (as opposed to mining for gold, copper, or silver, or printing on paper with ink), its production cost is essentially zero. In the future, and with a more technologically advanced world where money will be transferred between machines, and not from hand to hand, it will make a lot of sense to incorporate some type of cryptocurrency to handle these scenarios. Bitcoin is currently best poised to be this currency.

The second reason that Bitcoin will replace fiat money is that its value is not contingent upon world events. The Venezuelan bolivar is going down the drain? No problem. Mugabe in Zimbabwe wants to print more and more money? No worries! Bitcoin is relatively immune to these national policies because it is a worldwide currency.

Because the value of Bitcoin is spread collectively all over the world, what happens in one small country does not affect the value of Bitcoin much. However, if there's a systemic problem with Bitcoin that touches every corner of the world, then we will see investors running away from this cryptocurrency.

However, up until then, because Bitcoin transcends borders, there is a great incentive to use this currency to hedge against fiat currency is the local country. While this may not replace physical money worldwide, there would be a large contingent happy to keep their savings inflation free in Bitcoin, rather than seeing it wasted away in their local currency.

The final reason why Bitcoin may replace fiat currency is that **it seems to be the next level of the ascent of money.**

What do I mean by this? As we have seen, money once did not exist—we traded bushels of wheat for barrels of water. The transactions were slow and unique. This system of barter worked for a while, but soon we developed coins to represent a certain amount of money. These coins later were replaced with paper, and later with credit cards.

It seems like the next step in the evolution of money is for paper currency to be replaced with some type of cryptocurrency. Whether this means that it will be Bitcoin still remains to be seen, but the trajectory of money certainly is pointing in this direction.

ARGUMENTS WHY CRYPTOCURRENCY WILL NOT REPLACE FIAT CURRENCY:

There are also a few reasons as to why many believe Bitcoin will not replace fiat currency:

First in the list are banks and governments. These are the two institutions that will lose if Bitcoin, or any other cryptocurrency begins to compete with them, and they may put up a good fight to stop the rise of cryptocurrencies. Governments uniting together to halt the progress of Bitcoin because pounds, rials, dinars, and bolivars are losing remain a real enough possibility.

That said, it hasn't happened yet, but it's something to keep in the back of your mind if you're investing in this cryptocurrency.

Second, it takes just one instance of somebody using Bitcoin or another cryptocurrency to pay for drugs or any type of illicit behavior for the government to step in and create a reason for eliminating the cryptocurrency.

To attract the united ire and wrath of the United States Congress is not something cryptocurrencies should hope to do, especially if members from both parties are unhappy with the direction of Bitcoin. Cases such as these may allow dollars, euros, and rubles to remain in circulation much longer than we may anticipate.

This scenario would lengthen even further if bank workers, currency exchange workers, airport services, and financial accountants decide to unionize against the prevailing cryptocurrency winds. They may hold off the transformation of money from fiat currency to cryptocurrency because their jobs and careers are at stake.

CONCLUSION: IS IT TOO LATE TO GET INVOLVED?

It is never too late to get involved in Bitcoin investments. However, cryptocurrency investors must keep a few things in mind when investing in Bitcoin:

First: this is quite possibly the most erratic investment you will undertake. Over the few weeks that it took to create an outline for this book, Bitcoin's value jumped from $9000 to $17,000, just to plummet another $3,000 in fewer than four hours. Imagine for a moment losing $3,000 in four hours? You probably wouldn't be too happy.

According to Jethro Mullen from CNN Money, "trading has become especially frenzied in recent weeks as new investors have dived into the volatile market. Before Friday's fall, it had gained roughly $5,000 in the previous 48 hours (Mullen 2017)."[31] A high threshold for losing money is necessary for investing in Bitcoin, not only in its official value, but also in the platform you use, as there are many scams out there.

Mullen expands, stating that some "have gone bust altogether and others have suffered cyber heists in which hackers have made off with huge sums. The latest example is digital currency site NiceHash, where bitcoins worth more than $70 million were stolen this week" (Mullen 2017).

But what does Wall Street make of this? It appears that one of the largest drivers of Bitcoin's growth is that many Fortune 500 companies are looking to incorporate blockchain technology into their portfolios and long-term investments. Nonetheless, big banks "who have a complicated relationship with digital currencies – have issued a warning about the dangers of Bitcoin's future, saying the risks haven't been properly studied" (Ibid.). If banks unite to create a different cryptocurrency outside of Bitcoin, yet adopting blockchain technology, it may be a blow to Bitcoin's value.

Another attack on Bitcoin is coming from an unusual, yet growing, angle: environmentalists. Unlike physical currencies, Bitcoin isn't tied to any central bank. Instead, they are mined by computers with ASIC chips in "vast data centers that guzzle huge amounts of energy.

Bitcoin uses about 32 terawatts of energy every year (enough to power about three million U.S. households). […] By comparison, processing the billions of Visa transactions that take place each year consumes the same amount of power as just 50,000

---

[31] Quote taken from http://money.cnn.com/2017/12/08/investing/bitcoin-latest-price/index.html

American homes" (Shane 2017).[32] As we can see, attacks against Bitcoin have been coming from various angles, yet Bitcoin is still rising...

How do you get started?

Now that we got the bad news out of the way, let's make space for the good news. Here are some platforms and exchanges where you can buy and sell cryptocurrencies (especially Bitcoin) on the world market: **Coinbase, Kraken,** and **Bittrex**. There may be others, but you have to remain very wary of their ethical practices, as reports of scamming abound.

These three platforms seem to be much more legitimate than some of their counterparts. Investing in Bitcoin is inherently risky business due to the erratic nature of its value—the last thing you want is to worry about the integrity of the platform you're trading on. As always, speak to your financial advisor before investing in any cryptocurrency; we're only here to give you the most important information.

Bitcoin has grown tremendously over the past year—and this is just the beginning. While the value of Bitcoin is high (over $10,000), you don't need this much capital to invest. With the wallets and trading platforms named in this work, you can invest in a fraction of a Bitcoin stock.

Generally there is a limit to how little money you can invest, but these figures range in the tens or hundreds of dollars, not ten thousand. This means that the initial investor of Bitcoin could start off with investing only a twentieth of the a single bitcoin ($500) and potentially see it grow. More and more people are getting

---

[32] Information taken from http://money.cnn.com/2017/12/07/technology/bitcoin-energy-environment/index.html?iid=EL

excited about the promises of Bitcoin and the future of blockchain technology. With more enthusiasm comes higher values for cryptocurrencies, and Bitcoin, being no different plays by the same rules of the market.

Looking to the Future:

The future of Bitcoin and cryptocurrencies does look bright indeed. Clearly, Bitcoin has taken the lion's share of public scrutiny because of its amazing run in 2017, but the future of cryptocurrencies (including Ethereum, Ripple, and even Litecoin) looks quite promising.

As you can gather from the last few questions we answered above, we still don't know if Bitcoin is an anomaly in the cryptocurrency world or if it is here to stay. There are many uncertainties with Bitcoin, but **the one aspect of Bitcoin that seems to be more permanent and transferable to other industries is the use of blockchain technology.** This technology allows for linkages between many different industries that may begin to invest in it.

Bitcoin is the first currency to adopt blockchain technology as a tool for its operation. The benefits of blockchain technology permeate into banks, financial institutions, governments, and individuals. They may be able to adopt this technology in a relatively stable and hack-free manner.

As with any technology, it can be used for good and bad reasons. Bitcoin is no different. At the risk of sounding cliché, the future of Bitcoin is largely in the hands of those who decide to use it, meaning that it could be you.

GLOSSARY

ArcBit: a Bitcoin-based wallet where you could store your money.

Armory: a Bitcoin-based wallet used mainly for large institutions where you could store your money in cold or hot modes.

ASIC chips: application-specific integrated circuit chips used to mine Bitcoin.

Barter: original system of exchanging goods and services without mediums of exchange (money).

Bitcoin Cash: appearing from a hard fork in Bitcoin's blockchain; operating as a similar P2P and decentralized blockchain network without the oversight of a third party or centralized government.

Bitcoin Core: the original Bitcoin-based wallet; simplest and the wallet with the least amount of features.

Bitcoin Knots: the second iteration of Bitcoin-based wallets where you could store your money; more advanced than Bitcoin Core.

Bitcoin: first worldwide cryptocurrency adopting blockchain technology and capable of conducting payments in a digital fashion.

BitGo: a Bitcoin-based wallet used mainly for large institutions where you could store your money in cold or hot modes; allows for two-factor authentication.

Bither: a standard Bitcoin-based wallet where you could store your money; mostly for individual purposes.

Bittrex: a platform on which to trade Bitcoin and other cryptocurrencies.

Blocks: the foundational elements of blockchain technology; each block consists of a nonce, timestamp, root hash, and previous hash; all blocks are attached to each other through a chain.

Centralized ledger: original system of saving documents where all inputs and fiscal transactions are recorded into one supercomputer storing and maintaining all of the digital information of the network in one location.

Chains: the links binding blocks in the blockchain together;

relatively simple concepts compared to the block itself.

Coinbase: a platform on which to trade Bitcoin and other cryptocurrencies.

Cryptocurrency: any non-physical Internet-based currency; derived from the Greek word hidden (meaning *crypt-*) currencies, or mediums of exchange, incorporating complicated algorithms to encrypt data on a blockchain network; defining features of cryptocurrencies are their lack of palpability along with their adoption of blockchain technology.

Decentralized ledger: a middle ground between centralized ledgers and distributed ledgers, where supercomputers act as nodes for smaller networks of computers in a much larger network; considered safer than a centralized ledger, but not as safe as a distributed ledger.

Distributed ledger: a unique system that records documents onto every network account; implemented by every cryptocurrency using blockchain technology.

Electrum: a Bitcoin-based wallet where you could store your money.

Ether: the cryptocurrency developed by Ethereum to conduct transactions on a blockchain network.

Ethereum: a blockchain-based cryptocurrency that creates ethers as its currency; creates smart contracts for customers.

Fiat Currency: paper money currency in circulation and backed by the full force of the government.

FinTech: an abbreviated term for 'financial technology;' oftentimes considered as an approach rather than a system of governing currency exchanges.

GreenAddress: a Bitcoin-based wallet where you could store your money.

Hard Fork: a radical and complete alteration in protocols of cryptocurrencies rendering another set of transactions valid, similar to a valve on a faucet.

Kraken: a platform on which to trade Bitcoin and other

cryptocurrencies.

Litecoin: a cryptocurrency extremely similar to Bitcoin, yet with 84 million coins instead of the 21 million that Bitcoin would use; Scrypt computer coding language instead of SHA-256.

Mining: the electronic process by which Bitcoin is created; some cryptocurrencies do not allow mining (e.g., Ripple is pre-mined).

mSIGNA: a Bitcoin-based wallet where you could store your money.

Nonce: a random series of digits whose field value is fixed and unalterable so the hash complies with rules within the blockchain network; generally considered the zeros before a number.

Previous hash: the encrypted code, similar to the root hash, yet incorporating all of the codes from previous blocks; this hash indicates where the block originated.

Ripple: a cryptocurrency developed to facilitate interactions among financial institutions and eliminating needs for human interaction with currencies.

Root hash: a hash acting as proof that certain blocks were created; works as the identification of each block; goes by pseudonyms such as Merkle hash and Merkle root.

Scaling: the process by which a company can create 10 units of a product, and 10,000 units, with the same ease.

Scrypt: developed after SHA-256 and is considered the computer language for Litecoin.

SHA-256: computer language adopted by Bitcoin and other cryptocurrencies.

Smart contract: 21st century contract allowing for exchanges in property, money and financial investments in a 'live' fashion that does not need human interference or supervision; considered smart because it learns from itself.

Timestamp: perhaps the simplest part of the block in blockchain technology indicating when the block was created; timestamps cannot be altered or removed, creating another level of security for cryptocurrency users

Wallet: a place to store your cryptocurrency; purposefully simple term for what they really do.

Made in the USA
Monee, IL
01 January 2021